The Sounds of God

THE SOUNDS
OF GOD

Michael Mitton

eagle

Guildford, Surrey

British Library Cataloguing-in-Publication Data. A catalogue record for this book is available from the British Library

Published by Eagle, an imprint of Inter Publishing Service (IPS) Ltd, 59 Woodbridge Road, Guildford, Surrey GU1 4RF.

Printed by Thomson Press (India) Limited
Typeset by The Electronic Book Factory, Cowdenbeath.

ISBN No: 0 86347 067 X

Contents

Dedicated
to
Brother Ramon
whose life and ministry as a hermit have been a
constant source of inspiration and encouragement
to me in the writing of this book

Foreword

I first met Michael Mitton in 1981 through the pages of his impressive booklet *The Wisdom to Listen*. I sensed then that he and I were being led along parallel paths on our journey into God. Eight years later, I heard of him again when his appointment as Director of Anglican Renewal Ministries was announced. I rejoiced as I thought about this appointment. I sensed that he would bring to Anglican Renewal Ministries an exciting breadth of experience and spirituality since his theology was so clearly rooted in Scripture while displaying a delightful openness to the Holy Spirit and the freedom to explore contemplative prayer.

Shortly after the news of his appointment had been made public, the Elders of the church where I then worshipped were wondering who to invite to lead our annual parish weekend away. While we were listening to God together, the name Michael Mitton came into my mind. To our delight he accepted our invitation so subsequently he spent the entire weekend with our fellowship. For me the weekend was memorable for two things: Michael's wise, inspired and quietly authoritative teaching and the sense that here was a humble man who so obviously heard God that he awakened in others the longing to hear him too.

Since then Michael has re-visited some of the small groups who meet in that church and many people there would testify to the life-changing ministry they have received through him.

So when I was asked to become the Series Editor of these small books on prayer, I knew that I wanted Michael to be one of the contributing authors.

I was delighted when he accepted this further invitation and it fills me with joy to write the Foreword to his book.

Michael and I have met several times while the manuscript has been taking shape. On these occasions, our conversation has centred, not only around the contents of the book but on the Lord and ways of deepening our relationship with him as well. They have therefore been enriching and stimulating times for me and I have valued the level of sharing we have enjoyed.

The book has been an important one for me personally. I believe passionately that God is a God who speaks and that he pleads with us, his children, to listen to him. Yet it is so easy for the clamour of other voices, not least our own, to crowd him out and that is tragic because our lives then lose a sense of direction and our testimony to God's grace grows stale and lifeless.

But this book, laced as it is with Michael's characteristic humour and 'down-to-earthness' has created within me both a longing and a prayer. A longing to be more faithful in the discipline of listening to God with the whole of my being and a prayer that I might become ever more adept at hearing the God who uses such a variety of ways to communicate to us.

I believe this book is a timely one for today's church for three reasons. The first is that we live in a day when all of us are in danger of being driven by the 'muchness and manyness' of a multitude of so-called Christian activities instead of living from a still centre where God is free to reveal to us his plan for our lives. This book will help us to listen before we act and to act only when we have received our marching orders from God. The second is that I believe that God is constantly wanting to renew his church and that true renewal begins, neither with silence nor with exuberance but rather through being tuned into the voice of the God who longs to show us his plans for pouring new life into individuals, groups and churches. The third reason is that the contents could help evangelicals, charismatics and contemplatives to understand and trust each other. God has entrusted to each of those groupings a very important strand of spirituality. When they are woven together they make a wonderfully strong and attractive rope which will help us to scale many spiritual slopes and rock faces.

Joyce Huggett

They heard the sound of the Lord God as he was walking in the garden in the cool of the day, and they hid from him

Introduction

Then the man and his wife heard the sound of the Lord God as he was walking in the garden in the cool of the day, and they hid from the Lord God among the trees of the garden. But the Lord God called to the man, 'Where are you?'

(Genesis 3:8,9)

The first two chapters of Genesis depict a world in which God and his creation are in perfect harmony, and at the heart of this harmony we have free conversation between God and the man and woman. However with the terrible tragedy of the fall, this harmony is broken, and one of the dire consequences is that communication between God and his creation is damaged. From the intimate conversations of chapter 2, we now find Adam and Eve hiding from God, ashamed of their nakedness. Hiding among the leaves they hear the sounds of God walking in the garden in the cool of the day. The clear impression is that before the fall, God and his human creation would walk together in this garden of paradise in the cool of the day, discussing together their work and their play. Now this intimacy is broken. Now the man and the woman hide; but the encouraging thing is that the relationship is not entirely broken. They can still detect the sounds of God in the garden, and they hear the cry of his heart, 'Where are you?'

It could be reasoned that the coming of God incarnate to our world as the Word of God, and the sending of the Holy Spirit the divine communicator, would mean that the intimacy of the garden is instantly restored and man and woman once again would clearly and frequently hear the voice of God. But in our experience, if we are honest, this is not the whole truth. Yes, the coming of Jesus and the gift of the Holy Spirit has opened the gate of the garden to us. We need no longer hide among the leaves ashamed of our nakedness. We are no longer strangers, but we are beloved children who may discover God as 'Abba', and in so doing we can learn to communicate with him and listen to him. However, the hearing of God does not happen overnight. Indeed while we are here on earth, there will always be a 'now and a not yet' tension about hearing God. For now 'we know in part, and we prophesy in part, but when perfection comes, the imperfect disappears' (1 Cor. 13:9,10). When we enter into that garden that we call Paradise, we shall see him face to face, and we shall talk with him and stroll with him in the garden as we were always meant to. The wonderful hope set before us is that one day our Redeemer will return and God will come to restore this earth into a new heaven and new earth, and God will dwell among us after sin, death and the devil have been destroyed. Here we shall see face to face; here we shall understand fully, and we shall be in that place of perfection. Until then there is always going to be an 'in part' bit of our Christian life.

No more is this clearly apparent than in the business of hearing God. Much of listening to God is learning to detect the sounds of God while we go about our daily lives. For he has come to our world and our lives and moves about among us. This book is about discovering how we might hear those sounds and understand them. Within the sounds of God is indeed his voice, for he delights to speak to his children. My prayer is that those who read this book will discover new ways of detecting the sounds of God and hearing his voice, and that they will be taken further on in discovering more about God and the way he communicates to his people.

I would particularly like to thank Joyce Huggett who has been such an encourager to me during the writing of this book. I shall long remember trying to persuade our fax machines to talk to each other as chapters of this book were transmitted from Derby to Cyprus and back! My thanks also to the Anglican Renewal Ministries staff who sent me off for writing days and shouldered extra work as a result of my absence. Last, but not least, my affectionate thanks to my wife Julia and children who allowed me to disappear to my word-processor in our converted loft for hours on end and staved off writers cramp by ample measures of tea, coffee and my favourite chocolate biscuits.

The feast of Epiphany 1993

Chapter 1

The God of Sounds

In the autumn of 1991 I had the privilege of leading a mission to the chaplaincies of the French
Riviera, the highlight of which was a presentation
to the Archdeaconry Synod which took place at
Holy Trinity, Nice. The large Victorian church had
no sound amplification which meant that anyone
speaking in the church who wished to be heard
beyond the third row had to shout hard. So I began
shouting out my talk on renewal and vision when
someone at the back interrupted and said they could
not hear what I was saying. So I raised my voice to
a yell and continued my talk red-faced, perspiring
and exhausted at the end. I couldn't help feeling
that some of the more sensitive parts of the talk
had lost their impact by being delivered through a
yell! It also crossed my mind, as I returned to the
pew from whence I came, that my listening to God
was rather in this league. I can just about make out
his voice if he raises it to a yell, but anything less and
I am floundering. This, I hasten to add is nothing to
do with his voice which is perfect; it is to do with
my poor hearing and the poor acoustics of a fallen
world which often makes it difficult to catch what
God is saying.

I want to admit at the outset of this book that
I am writing as a learner and not as an expert.
I will admit that after years of trying to learn to
hear God better, I still stumble in the darkness and

go through times of finding it well nigh impossible to make out what he is saying. But there are other times when his voice is clear and I have little doubt that he has spoken. Hearing God has to be one of the most exciting, wonderful, yet awesome activities that we are permitted to experience. The more I hear the voice of God, the deeper my longing to hear more; the more I see the things of heaven, the stronger the yearning to see more.

There is a great sense of adventure when it comes to seeking the voice of God. This book will therefore be an adventure together. We are setting out on an exploration, seeking to discover effective ways of hearing our God who is in heaven, and yet who is also very present with us here on earth. Exploring is good fun so long as you don't mind making mistakes. I remember a few years ago, when as a family we lived in Yorkshire, one Sunday afternoon in a rather damp autumn, I had the sudden inspiration to lead the family on an expedition. Trusting Dad, they all dutifully and excitedly climbed into the car, and we drove to a place where a sign marked 'Public Footpath'. I had seen it earlier in the week and it looked exciting. So equipped with wellingtons and sticks and a small packed tea we made our way down the path, filled with the wonder and excitement of explorers. The confidence in the leader fell dramatically as the adventure went on, and it was not long before all the family were skidding and sliding in the most terrible mud, and Dad was trying to reassure the family as he clung to the baby, who was in danger of sliding down a mud bank into the river. Inevitably we came to a dead-end and we sat on a muddy bank and drank from our thermoses, with Dad trying to explain to Mum that life was about exploring, and the mud would probably come off if she used sufficient Persil. Strangely enough, despite the mud, the wet and the cold, the children always remember this as a joyful adventure! Children have that wonderful ability to enjoy and learn from adventure and exploration. As we explore the fascinating, complex and rather bewildering world of hearing God, we will need to catch the child-like spirit of adventure and not mind too much if we, metaphorically speaking, get a bit muddy on the way. For my family that particular expedition led us nowhere. But in our expedition in learning to hear God, I believe we will get somewhere, because God is utterly committed to seeing that we make progress in this area.

Why listen to God anyway?

We all know it is right to *talk to* God. As children we are taught that God likes it if we say our prayers. I am grateful for the discipline in my family of kneeling by my bed with father each night and saying some set prayers. They were comforting, and they established an invaluable discipline in my life. But it never occurred to me that God might want to talk back! I think I would have been shaken rigid if, following the Lord's prayer, a voice came from heaven saying, 'Thank you, Michael, now I have one or two favours to ask of you . . .' Somehow, speaking to God is safe. Even though it is a supernatural activity, it does not actually *feel* supernatural. It is normal. Normal church people do it. But the thought of God speaking back to us, brings in a whole new dynamic which is really quite disturbing.

I was a believer as a child, and I have loved Jesus

for as long as I can remember. But not until I turned twenty did it start to occur to me as slightly odd that every conversation I had with God was one way! I am sure one of the reasons I never listened to God was because I was a little bit afraid of him. It was when I was prayed for by a Pentecostal minister for that experience we sometimes call the baptism in the Spirit, that for the first time in my life I had a longing to hear God speak. I was no longer satisfied with the one-way conversation. Silence from heaven seemed far more painful to one into whom the love of God had been poured. My adventure began then in the early 1970s, and twenty years on I am still exploring, having made some exciting discoveries along the way.

In 1981 I wrote a booklet called *The Wisdom to Listen*.[1] There is a section in this book about listening to God, and as I wrote this section, for the first time I was forced to do some research on the subject. To do this research, I asked the basic question, Why do we need to listen to God? Very early on in my searching, I realised that hearing God is not just an option for those who are mystical and like that kind of thing. To hear God is absolutely crucial. In fact refusal to hear God is nothing less than life-threatening to our spirits.

The Bible makes it clear that God is a God who desires to communicate. If it does not sound disrespectful, he is actually very talkative, but not in the way we are usually talkative. We often talk long after saying what needs to be said. One of my bad dreams is that I am speaking to a group of people, and I have finished saying the useful things, but something within me feels I must fill up more time. I am on a kind of slippery slope of words, and I can't stop myself. As a result I talk rubbish, and I go on and on talking nonsense, and not surprisingly the poor victims who are listening gradually disappear from the scene, leaving me talking away still convinced I have to fill up the space. This is a very useful dream for me. It is a cautionary dream, where something deep within me has a horror of abusing words and of becoming trivial and meaningless, and so from time to time my subconscious sees the need for me to rehearse in my dream world what could happen in my real world if I didn't watch it.

Our own experience of speaking and listening to other people speaking does not really fill us with any great confidence about the subject of speaking. But then, from time to time, we are treated to the wonderful delicacy of a talk given by someone who has a respect for words. It does not have to be someone highly intelligent or qualified in the use of words and grammar – sometimes quite the reverse. But it is often someone who has learned to be still.

I imagine that God must have been still for all that time before he formed creation. In fact, the moment he spoke, something happened. Even in the midst of all that nothingness, all that time and timelessness, in the midst of that impenetrable darkness, God spoke – and the Bible story began.

In the beginning God created the heavens and the earth. Now the earth was formless and empty, darkness was over the surface of the deep.

(Genesis 1:1,2)

One of my hopes is that when we are in heaven, we will be allowed to travel back in time to have a look at the Creation. I cannot imagine a more spectacular or wonderful show. These first few verses of Genesis say so much with such a wonderful economy of words. There was God – right at the beginning. Out of nothing he created matter – he created our world, our little planet set in the infinite magnitude of space. But it had no form and there was nothing in it, and darkness was over the deep. This is a situation of utter tragedy – nothing but formless matter and dark depths. But then, the note of hope!

... and the Spirit of God was hovering over the waters (v.2)
Here we have a wonderful insight into the activity of the Spirit. Right here, in this deep, dark, formless world of tragic emptiness, the Spirit of God is at work, brooding like a dove broods over her nest. The Spirit is hovering, waiting for life. The Spirit is there, but unable to do anything until:

... And God said ... (v.3)
The moment God speaks, the Spirit moves in great and mighty power over this world, working as the power of God, making form out of formlessness, light out of dark, and bringing fertility to a barren land. Here, right at the outset, you have the involvement of the Holy Trinity – the Creator, the Word and the Spirit.

So with the story of Creation we learn something very important: when God speaks, things happen. When God speaks, there is creativity and life; when God does not speak, there is emptiness and darkness. If nothing else convinces us, then the story of Creation should put us in no doubt that if our lives are to be lives over which the Spirit of God may brood and bring light and life, then we must be those who will hear and receive the word of God.

Before the creativity of his ministry, Jesus also spent time in stillness. The Spirit of God came upon him at his baptism and drove him into the wilderness, and there in his encounters with the dark emptiness of Satan, he affirmed the Scripture, 'Man does not live on bread alone, but on every word that comes from the mouth of God.' (Deuteronomy 8:3)

He could not be clearer than that. Bread alone will not sustain us – we must feed from the word that proceeds from the mouth of God.

The Old Testament constantly affirms that God is a God who desires to speak. But there is no standard or set way that he speaks. Sometimes he speaks loud and clear, and at other times he speaks in a faint whisper.

Psalm 29 is a wonderful testimony to the sheer power of the voice of the Lord:

> The voice of the Lord is over the waters;
>   the God of glory thunders . . .
> The voice of the Lord is powerful;
>   the voice of the Lord is majestic.
> The voice of the Lord breaks the cedars . . .
> The voice of the Lord strikes with flashes of
>   lightning.
> The voice of the Lord shakes the desert . . .
> The voice of the Lord twists the oaks . . .

And I love the punchline in this Psalm:

> And in his temple all cry, 'Glory!'
>   (Psalm 29:3–9)

When you hear the voice of the Lord in this kind of way, there is only one appropriate response, and that is worship. There are times when the voice of the Lord is unmistakable. It is as loud as the thunderclap and as clear as the flash of lightning and as powerful in its effect as the mighty gale which twists great oaks. You cannot read this Psalm and say our God is a silent God. God has a great and powerful voice, a voice that sang creation awake, a voice that will be heard above the noise of a restless world.

But then there are times when God speaks in a whisper. I love the stories of Elijah – great stories of faith and fire. Elijah comes as the prophet of God to a sinful Israel which spiritually and morally has gone off the rails and is heading for disaster. He takes on false prophets, he takes on Ahab and he even takes on the dreaded Jezebel. The stories in 1 Kings build up to a great crescendo – the contest on Mount Carmel which is recorded in 1 Kings 18. Here again we are treated to a David and Goliath kind of contest – the good, faithful prophet of God against the evil king and his colluding cohorts. It is one prophet of God versus four hundred and fifty prophets of Baal. And here on this high place, the prophet of God is thoroughly vindicated. The fire of God falls on the sodden sacrifice, the people worship the true God and Elijah is given the task of slaughtering the four hundred and fifty false prophets. If the stories of Elijah finished here, then I think I would find this man of God always a bit unreachable. But I am comforted by the fact that Mount Horeb follows Mount Carmel.

Despite the great triumph of Carmel, Elijah is beset by fear. In the vulnerability of success and in the weakness of weariness he is overcome by fatigue and depression, and not far from Beersheba, a little way into the wilderness he finds a suitable juniper tree and seeks death (see 1 Kings 19:3ff.). And God speaks to Elijah. First of all he speaks through an angel, and then we are told 'the word of the Lord came to him' – the normal method for prophets to hear God. And Elijah is led to another mountain – Mount Horeb, the mountain of God. And here on this mountain of God, this man of God does what you or I do when we are afraid. He hides. He hides in a cave and we are told it is night. This is a desperate moment in Elijah's life.

Then came the wind, the earthquake and the fire and, I imagine very much to Elijah's surprise, the Lord was in none of these. The Lord, who had been so evident in the great and mighty acts of Elijah's ministry; the Lord who had sent fire from heaven to Mount Carmel; this same God was not in all this power and noise. But then comes the gentle whisper, and this completely disarms poor Elijah. We are told *a voice* speaks to him. It is not the familiar word of the Lord that Elijah knows about. It is simply a voice expressed in a whisper – a rather unfamiliar voice, yet one which Elijah understands as belonging to God. And here in this gentle whisper Elijah is told that his ministry is coming to an end, not in despair and depression, but in the promise of new things. And who knows, perhaps Elijah is given a glimpse of that other mountain he will visit – the Mount of Transfiguration where together with Moses he will meet with Christ.

We learn from these kinds of stories that God will speak both loudly and softly. We can expect times when he will raise his voice to a thunder, and there will be times when he will lower it to a whisper. The impression I get from this story is that Elijah discovered something new and very precious here – that God could be in a whisper. Even prophets have things to learn about listening to God! And there will be times for us – perhaps especially those dark times, when we are crying out for a word from the Lord, when we would dearly love to have earthquake, wind and fire messages from heaven – that we need to be especially open to the gentle whisper. If Elijah had failed to hear the whisper, then he would have missed hearing that crucial message about Hazael, Jehu and Elisha. We may not see ourselves as great prophets, but we are children of God, and here in these wonderful stories we see how God deals with his children. We will need to hear God in both the thunder and the whisper.

The Old Testament then is clear about the need to listen to God. It is also clear that failure to listen to him spells disaster. Listen to a typical warning in the book of Deuteronomy:

> So I told you, but you would not listen. You rebelled against the Lord's command and in your arrogance you marched up into the hill country. The Amorites who lived in those hills came out against you; they chased you like a swarm of bees and beat you down from Seir all the way to Hormah. (Deut. 1:43, 44)

Reading the history section of the Old Testament is in many ways quite agonizing. It is one story after another of people failing to listen to the Lord, and as a result there are countless stories of people being chased and taunted by swarms of enemies and disasters. The principle could not be clearer: if you listen to God and obey, he will bless; if you refuse to listen and disobey, you will be in trouble.

For some reason many in the church today think that the New Testament has changed all that. There is a kind of sense that it does not really matter any more. God is so loving and tolerant, that he won't really mind if we don't bother to listen. It is true that the New Covenant is to do with grace rather than law, but God's nature has not changed, and I am convinced that it is still as essential to listen to God today as it was in the days of Moses. We fail to listen to God at our peril, and when we look at the condition of our own spiritual lives and the spiritual health of the church, we must ask some probing questions about our ability to hear God. It is my conviction that one of the urgent and pressing needs of the church today is an ability to listen accurately to the voice of the Lord. The constant refrain in the first few chapters of the book of Revelation is, 'He who has an ear, hear what the Spirit says to the churches.' What is the Spirit saying to your church at the moment? What is he saying to the church denomination of which yours is a part? What is he saying to the church in this nation? What is the Spirit saying to the church in this world? There is no doubt that the Spirit is speaking, and we are called like the churches in the book of Revelation to hear what he is saying.

There are more ways than one

Most people have developed their own favourite way of hearing God and the way they choose is usually dependent on which particular stream of church life they come from. The danger is to settle into 'our way' of listening and not care for how other traditions do it. But part of the adventure is discovering that there are lots of ways to hear God. There are many different streams of life in the church. For the purposes of this book we shall look at three of these streams, namely catholic, evangelical and charismatic, and see what they have discovered about hearing God.[2] Let me just say something about each stream at the outset.

Catholic
By catholic I refer to the broad spectrum of spirituality that is found in the Orthodox, Roman Catholic and Anglo-Catholic traditions of the church. I know some will find this far too broad, but it will do for the purposes of this book. Catholicism has traditionally given a high value to the example of the saints, and to contemplative prayer.

Evangelical
By evangelical in this context, I shall be referring to traditional evangelicalism which finds representation in most of the major church denominations. Evangelicalism has given a high value to the Bible as the word of God and the supreme means through which God communicates to his world.

Charismatic
By charismatic I refer to that spirituality that particularly acknowledges the activity of the Holy Spirit, and gives a high value to experiences of the Spirit. Charismatics may worship in evangelical or catholic churches, but their distinctiveness for our purposes in this book, is that they would lay emphasis on hearing God through use of the activity and gifts of the Spirit.

I have not often consciously identified each stream as I write the book, as my hope is to weave together the strands rather than pull each out and examine it.

EXERCISES

1) Try and think back to a time when you clearly heard God speak to you. How did you hear him? How did it feel to hear God speak to you?

2) Who do you know who is good at hearing God. What is it about them, do you think, that causes them to be good listeners?

3) What is your main tradition – catholic, evangelical or charismatic? Why were you drawn to that particular tradition? What do you feel about the others? Are you willing to explore them a bit further in this book? Hold this all before God. If there is any sense of prejudice towards other traditions, ask God to cleanse you and give you an open mind. If you have been hurt in the past by one of these traditions, ask God to heal you, that you may be able to hear clearly, and not be coloured by hurts from the past.

Chapter 2

The Word of God

I can still recall that sense of excitement I used to feel as a young child when taken to the traditional Advent service of nine lessons and carols. In my mind I understood very little, but there was a magic about this service which got hold of my heart and imagination. Perhaps it was the fact that it marked the beginning of the Christmas season, which was for me a time of dreams and gifts, a time of being secure at home with all kinds of comfy and exciting feelings. We would drive to this evening service and find the church beautifully decorated. It was cold yet welcoming, and I enjoyed the extra candles whose lively flickerings complemented the immovable and solid pillars. The church was neither high nor low, but steered a middle course and therefore there was little variation in Sunday worship during the year. But at this carol service the church came alive. Here even the Vicar, much loved by our family, looked as if there was something flame-like flickering within his normal solid, and somehow unchangeable, exterior.

The lights would go out once the congregation had settled and a nervous cough at the back of church alerted us to the fact that our service was about to begin. The nervous cough belonged to one of the youngest choristers, whose privilege it was to sing the first verse of 'Once in Royal David's City', solo. I remember thanking God that I was not in the choir, and feeling eternally grateful that I did not have to endure this embarrassing ordeal of exposing my vocal chords, unaccompanied, to a full church which surely must be filled with music teachers who were just waiting to spot a stray note. But the ordeal over, the rest of the choir would join in, and the words of the great carol would fill the church from west to east, until finally we filled our lungs to proclaim the last verse which was all about our longing to see Christ return. Not that I had much clue about the Second Coming, but the music told me it was good news.

And so the service would proceed with extraordinary stories from the Old Testament and mysterious carols that only the choir knew, plus the familiar ones that I knew. Then, like some great crescendo, we would come to the final reading. The church would hush, and then some privileged member of the church would rise to the lectern and without announcement would go straight into that reading which seemed to sum up everything:

In the beginning was the Word, and the Word was with God and the Word was God . . .

It must have been years before I understood even the slightest bit of theology about this 'Word', and yet somehow instinctively within all the mystery of this service I knew that the Word coming to be among us was absolutely wonderful news.

Jesus – the Word of God

The opening to John's Gospel is like a re-write of the first chapter of Genesis. Here is another beginning,

The word was with God, and the Word was God

and it is to do with Jesus who is the Word of God, the Word who was present from the foundation of the world. Apart from the various technical meanings of this word, which is full of meaning for both Jew and Greek alike, by using the term 'Word' to describe Jesus, John is saying that one of the most important things about him is the message he carries. He is the Word of God. He is a message. The writer to the Hebrews puts it like this:

In the past God spoke to our forefathers through the prophets at many times and in various ways, but in these last days he has spoken to us by his Son, whom he appointed heir of all things, and through whom he made the universe. (Heb. 1:1,2)

For the writer to the Hebrews, as with John, one of the most important things about the coming of Christ to this world, was the fact that through him God would speak. God had indeed spoken through prophets, but now it is different. So concerned is God to communicate to us, that he sent his Son, Jesus, as the incarnate Word. Jesus therefore through his life, ministry, teaching, death on the cross, and resurrection, speaks powerfully to us, for he is the living Word of God. And he continues to speak. Jesus is the same yesterday, today and forever, which means that he is still the Word of God, and he still wishes to speak to us.

Jesus, as the Word of God, represents to us the way in which God likes to speak. We who are learners in hearing God, need therefore to study the Gospels and see how God communicated through his Son. Because the same Son will be communicating today, albeit not incarnate among us, he will presumably be speaking in much the same way.

When Jesus taught his disciples that he was the Good Shepherd, and they were like the shepherd's sheep (as recorded in John 10), he labours the point about the sheep becoming familiar with the shepherd's voice (see vv.3,4,16). The disciples will be characterised by their ability to hear the voice of Jesus. They will recognise his voice and be obedient to him. Even as Jesus spoke this parable it was being lived out there and then. The disciples knew this to be the word of God, and they listened attentively. John tells us that the 'Jews were again divided. Many of them said, "He is demon-possessed and raving mad"', and they go on to ask, 'Why listen to him?' (vv.19,20). The faithful sheep hear his voice, but there are sheep who do not, and by failing to hear the voice of the Good Shepherd they are in danger of behaving like wolves.

Jesus therefore expected his disciples to be those who would recognise and understand his voice. But even being with the incarnate Jesus day in and day out did not guarantee their being able to hear and understand him – it was not an easy business even then! There are a number of occasions where the disciples are completely baffled. Take for example the parable of the sower which is recorded in all three of the synoptic gospels. Here Jesus gives teaching about sowing the word. This is the story told by the Word of God about sowing the word of God.

Parables and puzzles

We are told by the Gospel writer Mark, that Jesus often used parables (Mark 4:2). I can imagine Jesus telling this parable about the sower scattering his seed over the land. And those who knew and loved the land would know just what he was talking about. They would know the frustrations of seeing valuable seed being plucked up by the birds. They would know the difficulties of that kind of terrain which was mostly rock and not much soil. They would watch hopefully as the seed grew up amidst the rocks, hoping so much it would find sufficient earth to root itself in, only to have their hopes dashed during a spell of hot weather in which they would see the promising young seed wither and die. Like all gardeners they would worry about the weeds. They planted their seed in what appeared to be nice clear soil, but as they carefully watered the crops they would see the unwelcome thorns and weeds growing with remarkable speed and energy, eventually suffocating the vulnerable seedlings. But it was all worth it for the seed which fell in the good soil. Here the farmer could come and see strong sturdy plants growing up without being destroyed by birds, rocks or weeds. So as Jesus spoke, the farmers in his audience would relate to the story well.

I sometimes wonder what happened when Jesus finished telling a story like that. If it had not been for the disciples pressing him, he would have left this story as a kind of riddle. I can see people in my mind's eye, straining to catch him as he spoke. It was all so familiar, and it was so comforting to know that this man, this rabbi, understood the aggravations of growing crops. But I can also imagine dismayed looks when Jesus stopped. According to the Gospel writers, Jesus is telling this parable by the lakeside. He is surrounded by a great crowd, and he uses a boat as a kind of platform. Then, when he finishes the parable, I imagine he gives the crowd a look which says, 'have you got the message?', and I imagine the majority of the faces in the crowd supported furrowed brows expressing profound puzzlement. And then it would all start up: 'Well, I have heard him before, and I am pretty sure he used a similar story to explain what death is all about – he talked about a grain of wheat falling into the ground and that . . .'

'Oh, I've got it – so the farmer is God, who gives life, but sometimes we have accidents and die . . .'

'that would explain the birds – they represent death'.

'Isn't there something in Daniel about that?'

'No, no, you're all wrong . . .'

And so it would go on. Now if I were there, I would be rushing up to Jesus and saying, 'They didn't get it – you've got to spell it out. You can't just paddle off in the boat and leave it in the air like this.' I'm glad one of the disciples had the honesty to ask why Jesus had to speak in parables. They were just as puzzled as the rest, and it is my theory that they spent at least half their time with Jesus, with dropping jaws and puzzled frowns, and if we were cartoonists we would probably draw a large question-mark over their heads. There were times when it was absolutely maddening being with Jesus – he would insist in talking in riddles. Why could he not just say 'I'm now going to tell you a story about the word of God; it has four main points, and I shall illustrate the points I am making by referring to a story about a sower'?

I suppose one obvious answer to this is that his teaching would have been terribly boring if he had! And one thing you could never say about Jesus was that he was boring. What was he doing by speaking in pictures? He was clearly saying something very important about the way God communicates to us.

In fact he does explain this just after the parable. The story in Mark goes on:

> . . . the Twelve and the others around him asked him about the parables. He told them, 'The secret of the kingdom of God has been given to you. But to those on the outside, everything is said in parables . . .' (Mark 4:10,11)

Secrets and sight

Here is the beginning of a clue. There are some secrets in the kingdom of heaven, and they are secrets there for the discovering. What is a secret? It is usually an important piece of information that is reserved for certain people. There are various kinds of secrets. We have lots of secrets in our home before Christmas, and a fair bit of my children's time is spent on trying to crack the secrets of what Mummy and Daddy will be giving them this year. My wife and I refuse to tell, because we want to wait for the right time. The right time is Christmas Day, which is the agreed day when the secrets will be revealed. So we keep some things secret from people, not because we don't like or trust these people, but because the time is not yet right for them to be revealed. And it is clear that God keeps some things secret from us, because it is not the right time for that particular part of his will or plan to be revealed.

As I write this I think of a meeting I had with my team just two nights ago. This is the nine of us who form the Anglican Renewal Ministries team. We had been talking together for a while about how we might develop the work in the immediate and long-term future. We then spent some time waiting on God, and one of our team shared with us a picture she felt God was showing to her. She sensed that we as a team were moving forward, but that we were surrounded by a thick fog. This fog was a God-given fog, and not one to be feared. Although it was difficult to make progress, it was a time of sharpening our eyesight and hearing. One of the reasons for God sending this fog was because we could not cope with the fuller vision if we were shown it. I daresay quite a number have received similar pictures as they have sought God about the future, and for us as a team we were encouraged by the fact that God would reveal his secrets to us, but only at the rate that we could handle. And this is often the way with revelation, and why the secrets of the kingdom are revealed slowly, some remaining secrets for an apparently long time.

But there is another kind of secret, one which is not revealed, not because the bearer of that secret is unwilling to reveal it, but because the hearer is unwilling to receive it. And Jesus speaks about such people in Matthew's version of the sower story:

In them is fulfilled the prophecy of Isaiah:
'You will be ever hearing but never
  understanding;
  you will be ever seeing but never perceiving.
For this people's heart has become
  calloused; they hardly hear with their
  ears, and they have closed their eyes.
Otherwise they might see with their eyes,
  hear with their ears,
  understand with their hearts
and turn, and I would heal them.'
But blessed are your eyes because they
  see, and
  your ears because they hear.
                                    (Matt.13:14–16)

Jesus here is talking about eyes and ears of the heart. There are people, he is saying, who have eyes and ears, who can see and hear, but their hearts are overgrown with all kinds of things, so that althought they can see and hear outwardly, they cannot see and hear inwardly. The language that Jesus speaks is one that is for hearing inwardly. The visions Jesus shares are ones that can be seen with the eyes of the heart. Paul probably has this in mind when he prays for the Ephesians, that the eyes of their hearts may be enlightened.

In the crowd surrounding Jesus on the lakeshore would be those who would have open and receptive hearts ready to learn from Jesus, but there would also have been those with calloused hearts. For the open-hearted, there would be revelation. They might have to work at it, and chew on it for some time, but in time they would hear and understand, and see and perceive. But there were those whose hearts were calloused by harsh doctrines, prejudice and pride. For them the things of the kingdom would always remain a secret, and the doors to healing, closed.

I sense so much sadness in Jesus when he uses this prophecy from Isaiah. He was so grieved, as well as angered, to see those who should have had such clear 'heartsight', causing others to stumble because of their own blindness. John records a lengthy discussion in chapter 9 of his Gospel about this blindness that is so evident in the Pharisees.

But it must have been deeply comforting to the disciples to have heard Jesus say to them, 'Blessed are your eyes because you see, and your ears because they hear'. (Matt. 13:16)

The parable of the sower assures us that God is always wanting to scatter his word. There is a sense here of carefree generosity. God is not stingy with his word – there is plenty of it, and he freely gives it out. The problems come in receiving it. We receive the word of God in the earth of our hearts. There is the place for it to settle, take root, grow and bear fruit many times over. But the warning in this parable is that all kinds of things can threaten the life of the word of God in our hearts. Satan is around like those menacing birds to pluck the word out as soon as it is sown. There is the risk that the seed may only lie near the surface. This is the kind of situation where we have not developed depth in our hearts – we live life at a superficial level, so nothing is allowed to penetrate. If the word of God is to take root, we

The seed in the good soil bears fruit many times over

must provide depth, and that comes from spending time with God in worship, stillness, dwelling on the things of God. Otherwise when persecutions come, the seedling withers. Then there is the threat of the weeds. The weeds represent those things which can take root in our hearts and, far from producing good fruit of the kingdom, produce thorns and cast the good seedling into the shadows. Jesus tells us that the weeds are things like materialism, which will always have the effect of hardening the heart. But the very reassuring thing about this parable is that despite the fall-out, a lot of the seed does take root and flourish.

Now all this tells us quite a lot about the way God communicates with us:

1) We should not be surprised if God speaks to us in riddles and parables. In the book of Numbers, the Lord speaks to Moses, Aaron and Miriam about how he will communicate (see Numbers 12:4–8). He will speak to Moses face to face but he is the exception. To others, he will speak through visions, dreams and riddles. In the New Testament we see this continued, Jesus often communicated with this kind of language. In fact, the disciples rarely got a straight answer out of him, and so it is unlikely we will!

2) We must give time to getting to know the voice of the Good Shepherd. We will not hear his voice unless we get close to him. Many are like sheep afraid of the shepherd, so they keep their distance, and of course will always find it hard to hear God. It is not easy to listen to someone of whom we are afraid. It is often the experience of those who come into a renewal of their faith by the power of the Spirit, that they are led into a new intimacy with their Father in heaven, for it is the Spirit of God who causes us to

cry 'Abba, Father' (Rom. 8:15). The Spirit draws us into the intimacy of the Trinity, and it is here that we can dare to believe that our Good Shepherd longs to speak to us.

3) We need to recognise the fact that we will receive the seeds of the word of God in good soil, and this is the uncalloused heart. This means we will have to allow God to work on our hearts. If our hearts are full of sin, they will be hardened and will not hear. Please don't think this implies that all failure to hear God is due to our personal sin, but we should take note of the fact, that it is in the region of the heart that we hear God. It is the pure in heart who see God (Matt. 5:8), and it is the one who has clean hands and a pure heart who can ascend the mountain of the Lord (Psalm 24:4).

The Bible as the word of God

One of the great contributions of evangelicalism has been to constantly emphasise that the Bible is not simply a humanly-inspired document, but it is indeed the word of God. Evangelicals appreciate the Bible as the inspired, inerrant, authoritative word of God. It has a unique right to be heard as God's word to his world today. Evangelicals have a great love for the Bible. Evangelical preachers will favour expository preaching, taking a book from the Bible and working their way through it over a number of sermons. An evangelical church will be characterised by an open Bible in the pulpit. In an Anglican church, you can often tell from the architecture of the building whether or not it was built in the evangelical tradition. I remember once coming across a church in Leicestershire where the altar (known in evangelical churches as 'the Lord's table') was a tiny little thing tucked away in a simple east end, but in the middle of the church was an enormous pulpit which spoke majestically of the power and authority of the word. I think nowadays such an architectural statement about the authority of the word would seem rather over the top, but clearly at the time of construction, those who built this church wanted to make a point.

A back light and theology

The evangelical will also be an avid Bible reader, and a much loved and well worn Bible will never be far away. I remember hearing that fine evangelical leader and expositor from St. Ebbe's Oxford, Keith Weston, leading a University Christian Union weekend for us when I was a student. He spoke of his pocket New Testament as a 'back light' because he always kept it in his back pocket. So impressed was I that I immediately went out and bought myself a nice black pocket RSV, which I tried with considerable use of force to place in my jeans back pocket. I successfully inserted it, but found I was unable to sit down with any comfort whatsoever! Out of necessity my 'back light' soon became a coat-pocket torch, and before long it became well-worn, underlined, annotated and highlighted.

I had two main Bibles when I was a student. There was my much-loved RSV (*Revised Standard Version*), covered in 'Jesus stickers' and used at Christian Union meetings. Then there was my study Bible, a Revised Version. It was a rather fine hard-back copy that I picked up for 2 shillings in a second-hand bookshop. This was the Bible that accompanied me to the theology faculty for my lectures. One Bible represented my evangelical devotion; the other represented my studies for a degree in theology. Exeter University at that time boasted of having one of the most liberal theological faculties in the country. My first Old Testament essay was entitled, 'Pentateuch, Tetrateuch, Hexateuch. Discuss in the light of form criticism, literary criticism, and traditio-history.' My evangelical background had not prepared me for this! I still have the essay and scrawled across it in bold red ink were remarks from the tutor like 'You have come to University to think' and 'You must get rid of your fundamentalist presuppositions'. Needless to say I failed that essay and the next one.

During my first year I lived with a split personality. I would not let go of my evangelical love for the Bible, and yet I feared being ridiculed by the lecturers. These were the high days of liberalism. Any idiot could see that evangelicalism was for the simple. The Christian Union was for those who were simplistic in their faith and who would not face the real issues. The Christian Union, fostered by the Inter-Varsity Fellowship (now UCCF) viewed the theological faculty with great suspicion and saw it as being full of liberals, and people like me should be prayed for, that we would get through the three years with our faith intact. Sadly it was true that some fine young Christian men and women did arrive at University to read theology and to learn more about their Lord, only to see their faith unable to stand the rigorous questionings and searchings of liberalism.

By my second year I was starting to enjoy my

theological studies immensely. Academically, school had been rather a disaster for me, with poor results at A level. When I came to the interview I presumed I would not be offered a place because of my low grades. However Professor Roy Porter, with characteristic lateral thinking, astonished me by saying, 'Well Mr. Mitton, I see that you are very bad at English, Economics and Maths, as your A level results reveal; I can only assume you will be very good at Theology', and with that he offered me a place! I was so grateful for this opportunity, for here I found a subject that I loved, and I managed to get my degree. More importantly, God was at work in my life during those three years, deepening my love for the Bible, but at the same time making me unafraid to question and probe. I no longer took it as a personal attack that someone should suggest that the book of Isaiah might have had three authors. In fact to me, this made good sense, although it was against party-line.

I emerged from University with a deeper and more mature love for the Bible, and it was indeed a means through which I heard God speaking to me. I no longer felt so much at home in traditional evangelical settings, and the liberal influence on me together with my charismatic experience meant that I could no longer be neatly categorised as a conservative evangelical. But nonetheless, many of my evangelical convictions had been strengthened, and my love for the Bible was steadfast.

The power of the word

It is the testimony of countless Christians down through the centuries that the Bible has been a means through which they have heard the voice of God. There are all sorts of famous examples of people being converted through reading the Bible. As they encountered the words on the pages, so they met the Living Word. The great Augustine attributes his conversion to the little child who, outside his garden wall, cried 'take up and read', and Augustine picked up a copy of the Bible that was next to him and started to read and thereafter served Christ. The risen Christ appeared to the two disciples on the road to Emmaus, and he opened the Scriptures to them so that their hearts burned within them. The evangelist, Philip, having been instructed by the Spirit to walk alongside a chariot in the desert, meets a eunuch who is reading Isaiah. It is Philip who explains the Scripture to this distinguished Ethiopian, who is converted and baptised.

On my own journey of learning to hear God speak I find myself holding on firmly to the conviction that the Bible is the word of God. I love to read it. It is food and drink to my soul, and I feed from it every day. My usual devotional practice is to follow the Anglican lectionary (a programme of morning and evening Bible readings that many Anglicans use). I say the short service of Morning Prayer by myself, and generally make use of the Old Testament and New Testament readings as set for the day, together with the Psalm. I enjoy using this structure as it means a lot to me to be in fellowship with other Anglicans who will be following the same readings in their homes and parishes. It is often during the reading of the Psalm that I start to engage in discussion and prayer with God. Perhaps I have come to my morning prayer concerned for a friend who is in need. Then I read one of those Psalms which cry out for God to do something. At these times, it comes alive for me. Not only do I feel God has comforted me, but I make use of it in intercessory prayer. The Psalms are so full of feelings. How disappointing it is when they are intoned in a monotonous way that ensures they are emptied of feeling.

When I begin my morning readings, I am usually somewhat weary, and despite having been for a ten-minute jog round the block, there is little to suggest that I have woken up. But I enjoy the experience of knowing that even if there are not blinding revelations, just to read the words of the Bible feeds my soul. Sometimes it seems right to pause and meditate on a particular phrase, rather as one would savour a particular flavour in a special dish. At other times I get caught by the feel of the passage. As I write this I am reading through the book of Revelation. If I'm honest I have very little idea what some sections are about, but I feel a stirring in my spirit. I can make contact with the great crescendos of praise, or the heartfelt cries of the angels.

God speaks to us through his word. He has spoken to us through his Son, who is the Word of God, and he speaks through his holy word, the Bible. In the next chapter we will look in more detail about how God uses his word to speak to us.

EXERCISES

1) *Spend some time thinking about the parable of the sower in Mark 4:1–20. Use this to look at your own heart. How receptive is it to the word of God?*

2) *How does Satan steal the word of God away from your heart?*

3) *How can you become a deeper person, so that the seed won't remain at a superficial level*

4) *What are the weeds that suffocate the seed as it grows within you?*

Allow time for the Holy Spirit to heal, and to deepen his work in your heart today, so that the eyes of your heart may be opened.

Chapter 3

Hearing and Words

Hearing God and faith

Occasionally you come across people to whom God has spoken with an audible voice. For seven years I was a Vicar in the Worcestershire town of Kidderminster. Early on during my time there I met Beryl. Beryl's daughter had been married in our church, and not long after the wedding, Beryl met Jesus. She had not been particularly keen on God during much of her life, but she was a woman with a lovely open heart. One day, quite out of the blue, she had a Damascus-Road experience of encountering Jesus, in her small council house on the edge of town.

Beryl very much enjoyed those early months of getting to know Jesus. She sensed his presence, and she began to learn to hear his voice. On some occasions she heard him speaking so clearly that it was as if someone else in the room had spoken to her. Perhaps the most dramatic example of this was early one morning when she heard him speak to her. Beryl was a smoker, and despite some gallant attempts she had failed to give it up. She sometimes felt guilty when among Christians who gave those sideways glances of disapproval at her shopping bag which revealed a packet of Silk Cut. I remember saying something to the effect, 'Beryl, when you are strong enough and can manage without, God will help you give up smoking.' She accepted this, and gave up trying, and for the most part gave up feeling guilty. Then on this particular morning, she followed her usual custom after waking up of reaching for her Bible and her packet of cigarettes. As she lit up, she heard a voice that said, 'That is your last cigarette.' And it was. God had spoken loud and clear, and such was the force of it that it caused Beryl to give up a life-long habit.

Now all those who have a problem with smoking immediately think to themselves, 'Why can't God speak to me like that'. The fact is God will insist on being God and doing things his own way. There are many examples of people hearing God through an audible voice, through visions or from angels. But for the most part God speaks to us when we read the Bible, through hearing a sermon, through friends or books, or just inner impressions received in that intuitive place within us. So if God is able to speak through such unmistakable ways, why does he choose, more often than not, to speak through the more cryptic ways? One of the reasons is so that we can grow in faith.

When it was first suggested that I consider applying for the post of Director of Anglican Renewal Ministries I more or less rejected the idea out of hand. I was happily settled in my work, I enjoyed working in the Worcester Diocese and was hoping to stay in that Diocese for some time, and I had no sense that it was right to move out of parish ministry. My wife, Julia, and I discussed it briefly and both agreed that God would have to speak very powerfully if he wanted us to move. That evening, before going to sleep we read the evening readings in 'Living Light' (a book of selected Bible readings from the Living Bible for morning and evening each day of the year). The opening verse shook me rigid: 'Abraham trusted God, and when God told him to leave home and go far away into another land which he promised to give him, Abraham obeyed' (Heb. 11:8). Here in these few simple words, my life was to be set on a different course.

There followed several months of heart-searching, of discussions with friends, of prayer and seeking. Throughout this time, and indeed throughout my time of working with Anglican Renewal Ministries, Abraham has been for me an important role model of faith. He heard God speak to him. He had learned to hear the voice of God, and even though God told him to do something humanly ridiculous, he believed. He believed God could provide a nation from his barren wife, Sarah. He believed God could provide a fertile land out of drought-stricken Palestine. Despite one or two wrong turnings, Abraham remained on course. God had spoken, and he would obey.

God could have sent a dazzling angel to Kidderminster that day saying to me, 'Michael, the Lord has called you to work for Anglican Renewal Ministries.' I would be in absolutely no doubt that God had called me, and in many ways I would have no further cause to discuss the matter with him. But God is always wanting to develop our relationship with him, and over the subsequent months following this Abraham verse, I spent time with God, searching and listening for his voice, and it was from having spent time in this intimate place with him, that the certainty of the call came to light.

Faith is utterly essential when it comes to hearing God. We approach God's word in faith, expecting to hear his voice. When God speaks to us, we immediately enter into that internal interrogation, (Was it God or was it me? Was it really his voice?), but that very process of investigation takes us into deeper places of faith. Once we have discerned that it is his voice, we hold on by faith. We take action on it in faith.

If I were to try and summarise what the last few years in my life have been about, I would say this time has been for me all to do with lessons in faith. It has been about learning to be prepared to walk near the edge and to trust God.

Hearing through the Bible

Once we have accepted that God speaks through his word, how does it actually work? How do we hear God speaking to us about particular situations?

Most people develop their own favoured method and I am always reluctant to recommend one in particular. A general foundation is that regular reading of God's word will mean that we will always have a pool of remembered Scripture within us. At any time the Holy Spirit might bring this to mind to help guide us. I find quite often when I am praying for someone, God brings to mind a verse or passage from Scripture that I have read in recent weeks, and I can use it to minister to that person. I have also known many occasions where my morning reading has been remarkably apt for someone I am with, and it develops a prophetic dimension.

I'll come clean and own up to the fact that the way God often speaks to me is by referring me to Bible references. These are references which I don't recognise, but when I look them up they can be very significant. I think one of the reasons why God chooses to speak to me through this means is because I used to be so snooty about it. I would always quote the man who was in a desperate situation and asked God to speak. He felt he heard God give him the verse Matthew 27:5. He was dismayed to find the verse read, 'Judas went away and hanged himself'! This story is told often as an obvious example of the weakness of this particular method.

But then as I thought about this, I began to wonder why God was not allowed to speak in this particular way. This method would only fail if we were not prepared to make mistakes and use our common sense. It came as quite a relief to discover that I might actually be able to say to the man who turned up Matthew 27:5, 'Perhaps you got it wrong'! From somewhere Christians have got hold of the notion that when we listen to God, whether it be through the Bible, through gifts of the Spirit or whatever, we must always expect to hear it right, and fully right. The fact is that most of my listening is a mixture of my voice and God's, and maturity comes with learning to distinguish.

There have been some very important times for me when God has referred me to Bible verses. During 1991 I began to sense that God was calling us to produce a course on evangelism. To shorten what is quite a long story of faith, by early 1992 plans were underway to produce *Saints in Evangelism,* using J. John as the author. We also felt directed by God to make this course a video, and made use of Mike Pritchard, an excellent Christian film-producer. The filming day was at the end of March. We launched a fund to raise the thousands of pounds necessary to pay for the production. We wrote to trusts, applied for loans and so on. With about six weeks to go, we still had very little in the account and I could feel panic arising within me. I knew ultimately this had been my vision and I was responsible. In six weeks we would need a great deal of money. Our bank accounts were more or less dry and we had got a long way behind on the payment of some big bills. If I had heard God wrong on this, I was committing Anglican Renewal Ministries to financial suicide, and I would put all those working on the project in difficulties. But we could still pull out and cut our losses.

J. John, Mike Pritchard and I met at St. Alkmund's Church, Derby, to do some planning for the filming. Now it was real, it was no longer on the drawing-board. There was, paradoxically, a great sense of excitement about the project, but also within me I know fear had reared up and sent all faith fleeing. It was as though I had been walking on the very edge of my faith, but now I had fallen over into the chasm of fear. Inwardly I plunged, while keeping a brave face on the outside. Just before I left the church, Paul Corrie, the Vicar of St. Alkmund's sensed I was not quite right. He took me into the chapel.

'Are you all right?' he asked

'Yes, I think so,' I lied

'Are you really all right?' he pursued

'No. I'm absolutely terrified!'

It was a relief to have Paul there, with whom I could own up to my fear and from whom I would receive no condemnation. I spent the evening phoning some of our prayer partners. Paul had agreed that I could speak to the church on Sunday. My plan was to ask people to pray for us, to help us discern what God was saying. I was going to share with them my concern that I might have heard God wrong. My real anxiety was that what I had heard had not been the voice of God, but simply the voice of my own ambition. I was scared that *Saints in Evangelism* was not a calling from God, but was a bright idea of Michael Mitton, that had little to do with the kingdom of God.

On the Sunday morning Julia and I awoke a little earlier than usual. Julia was on ministry-team this day, so she wanted a little time to prepare and listen to God. I noticed she had got out her *Living Light* readings. Not to be outdone I got out my *Living Light* as well. There we were, sitting in bed sipping tea and both trying to listen to God. I was trying to work out how I would speak to the church, when I sensed God say to me, 'Turn to March 24th. I have something to say to you through this.' I dutifully turned it up, again going through that process of wondering whether it was me or God. When I saw the leading verse, I knew it was God: 'Abraham believed God; then God considered him righteous on account of his faith . . . Abraham never doubted. He believed God for his faith and trust grew ever stronger. He was completely sure that God was able to do anything he promised . . .' and so the readings went on. I felt a strange quietening going on within me, like that point in a storm when you know it is starting to wane, and there are even signs that the clouds are parting as you glimpse rays of light among the hitherto darkened watery mass.

I turned to Julia and said, 'God has spoken to me through this passage.' As I read it out, she shut her copy of the book, and a leaf came loose and floated down on to my lap. I picked it up and passed it back to her. She searched for the place as I finished reading the Abraham passages of faith. When I finished she said, 'Look what date this page is.' Sure enough it was 24th March, the very page I had been reading from in my version of the book. Never before had a text of Scripture literally leaped out at me!

I spoke to the church that day, but it was no longer to ask them to pray for guidance. I apologised for my lack of faith and trust in God, and that now I knew that God had sealed this project with his word. I asked them to join me in prayer that God would provide all that we would need in time for payment. You can imagine the delight in the office that week when two substantial gifts came in and a loan was offered. Soon after that two other large gifts arrived, and by the filming-day all the major bills were covered.

When we learn to hear God, we will be on a journey of faith. Like Abraham I wavered, but God steered me back. The waverings are all a part of it.

As we approach the Bible as a means through which God chooses to speak to us, it is good to ask God to direct us to a familiar way of hearing him through his word. Ignatian spirituality offers a lot of help with this. Here we are invited to enter into a Bible story and imagine ourselves involved in that story. I have often found leading such meditations has been a help to people in their listening to God. For example, if I am preaching on the story of the healing of the woman with the haemorrhage (Luke.8:43–48), I might take a few moments at the end of the sermon to guide people through a meditation built around the story. I would ask them to imagine that they are like that woman, and to recognise places within themselves where they are feeling drained and weary and unhealed. They may well be in that situation of having tried everything, but they are confused. But now they have an opportunity to meet with Jesus. Jesus is not too busy to spend time with them. Here is an opportunity to make contact with him. And in some moments of quietness I would ask people to be open to hearing

Jesus speak personally to them. As people get inside these wonderful Gospel stories, they very often meet with Jesus in a powerful and healing way, and hear his voice.

Hearing God through the sermon

John Hadley in his book, *Bread for the World* writes about the ministry of the word in the Eucharist:

> But now a reassuring moment: breath is taken, throats are cleared, chairs scraped; the ritual grinds to a halt, and at last (as long as the translation is lucid, the reader audible, and the microphone is working) here comes something apparently straightforward: the reading of Scripture. This is the word of the Lord! for us all to mark, learn and inwardly digest; straight talk from on high; marching orders for the week ahead.'

He goes on to talk about the sermon:

> As with Scripture itself, as later with the gifts of bread and wine, so God can take the preached word and speak through it, breathe fresh life into it, make Christ present in it. Here again the word is spoken uniquely to each listener: most preachers have the experience of being warmly thanked – or upbraided – for something in a sermon that was never intended, or quite misunderstood, or taken out of context, or blown up out of all proportion. 'But that isn't what I

was saying at all!' Maybe not; but maybe that is what God wants them to hear.[2]

For evangelicals the sermon is the high point of the Eucharistic service; for the catholic, the sermon is one of the steps along the way, the high point being the Communion. Perhaps we have missed something important by creating high points in the service. God is active and at work at all points during the service, and we may hear him at any point.

But the sermon is a very good opportunity to listen to God. As John Hadley points out, God does have an astonishing way of saying things through us preachers that we never thought we said! This says quite a lot about the activity of the Holy Spirit during the sermon. The Spirit is always active, communicating the truth to us. When we come to listen to a sermon therefore, we should be prepared and listening for whatever God has to give us.

Some of us are fortunate to attend churches where there is a high quality of preaching. We can go to church on a Sunday and feel fairly confident that God will speak to us through the preacher. Others however may feel that the sermon is not exactly the high point of the service! Without casting any aspersions, it would not be untrue to say that there are many preachers around who lack some basic communication skills. There are also many who communicate vagueness and muddledness. This is not intended as an attack on preachers, but to make clear that I understand how it feels for those who have to listen. My present work does not involve regular Sunday duties, so I am more often than not, sitting in the pew rather than at the clergy desk on a Sunday. After fourteen years of ministry, this has been an excellent experience, and my preaching has changed as a result.

Hearing God through a lively and inspired sermon is not difficult. Many is the time when I have felt spoken to by God during the course of a sermon. But what if I am not so fortunate and the sermon is not particularly inspiring? If this is the case, then I have to develop a discipline. The discipline begins by praying for the preacher. I must pray for him or her as they prepare during the week. Pray that they will be gripped by the Bible text they are studying; pray that the word will reach not just their brain but their heart; pray that their heart will burn within them while Jesus opens the Scripture to them.

When it comes to listening to the sermon, I will need to open my mind fully to the inspiration of the Spirit. This will involve surrendering any sense of judgement or resentment I may feel towards the person preaching. It is most unlikely that I will hear God with resentment gnawing at my heart. If the sermon is rather like a confused knot of threads, I like to try and find one of the threads that is alive for me. I have found quite often that there is something that the preacher says which is like a thread. It may be rather confused, but I invite the Spirit to draw it out from the knot. I don't think it matters that our mind 'wanders', and many could testify to the fact that they missed the rest of the sermon as some important message was privately pursued. I would far sooner a person had heard one important thing that they could apply in their lives, than that they had heard the whole sermon and left church untouched by it.

People only remember one or two points from a sermon even if they listen to the whole lot. It is far better to do something creative with one thread, than to exhaust ourselves by concentrating on the whole thing. Once we have recognised the thread we can let the Spirit make it into the means through which God speaks to us. It then becomes a thread of life which we can use to weave into the wider fabric of God's ongoing word to us at this time. In this way, even the most confused preacher can be the messenger of God's word to us.

Hearing God and reading

It's easy to go into a Christian bookshop and become cynical about the sheer quantity of books. A week never goes by without our office receiving a new book for review in our magazine. You can go into Christian bookshops and spend hours looking through book after book. You can learn how to pray with the rosary; you can read about revival in China; you can solve your marriage problems and you can get your doctrine of hell sorted out. There seems to be no limit to it, and sometimes I sit down and ask myself, 'Why do we do it? Why do we keep on writing more books? Haven't we got enough now?'

But then as I think more about it, I realise that each time someone writes a book, they are writing it because they have been attempting to listen to God. They are learning something about God and his world, and they have learned something which they feel is worth sharing. As you browse in the bookshop, you home-in on a particular book that you like the look of because it might help to make sense of a particular part of the journey you are on. It has a great potential for being the means through which God can speak to you. The fact that there are so many books on the market speaks of the release of creativity that there is in the church at the moment. God is speaking to his people about many things. We must guard against indiscipline, but we must encourage creativity.

There have been times in my life when I have picked up a book and it has profoundly influenced me. God has spoken at that moment to me so clearly. I pick it up a year or two later and it has 'gone dead'. It is therefore essential that we choose carefully what we read. We should shun 'fashion reading', where we read one of the top ten books just because everyone else is reading it and we want to be fashionable. Yes, at times there are books which are prophetic in nature and have something to say to the whole church at a given time. But generally speaking we should read those books God is calling us to read. There are many books I am told that I should have read, but probably never will. I try and discern what is the book God is giving me at this moment which will bring me life and bring his word to me.[3] Once we have found the book that is right for us, how do we read it in such a way as to hear the voice of God?

Much depends on how we approach it. I have an almost uncontrollable urge to get through every book in the fastest possible time. I find myself taking note of where the chapter ends and say things like, 'I should just be able to finish this chapter before . . .' as if the sole purpose of reading the book is to get to the end of it. We can then devour another with equally impressive speed and on it goes. But when I get into this frame of mind I rarely get inspired. I have to learn to slow down and treat the book with respect. I need to read a bit, and then have time out for thinking. I like to make notes in the margin, or mark bits that mean something to me. If

I sense God speaking clearly to me through a book, I will probably go back to that book several times and digest it deeply into myself so that God can do all he desires to do through it.

A useful exercise before starting each chapter is to ask the Holy Spirit to speak to me and to point out anything in this chapter that I need to take particular notice of. If I do pray this, then I must be prepared to stop in a lay-by, so to speak, to then spend time with God in conversation about the particular thing he is pointing out to me. This may mean that it could take a long time to read a book! But surely it is far more worthwhile to read one book well, than to race through ten and not have learned anything.

Respecting words

There is no doubt that our God is a God who speaks through words. Some, like the young Samuel, may hear the voice of God speaking with words directly to their ears. For Beryl, mentioned at the beginning of this chapter, this experience changed a life-long pattern. For all of us, we have the gift of the Bible, God's holy word to us, through which we can learn to listen to him. God has given his church preachers and teachers whose words may become the means through which he speaks to us. God has also released writers to his world, through whose words we may also hear the sounds of God. Again, there are no easy techniques to offer, but there is an attitude to develop. This is the attitude of respecting words. And the way to respect the words I receive, is to respect the way I use words in my own speech.

One book that I often go back to, and which

for me has been full of many lay-by's, is David Runcorn's *Space for God*. In this book he describes his experience of a time of solitude in an alpine cabin. He writes this:

> During my own time of silence in the alpine cabin, I experienced what felt like a complete collapse of language. It was as if I had been making words work so hard that now in the silence they fell away from my control, exhausted and emptied of meaning . . .
>
> Through it all I became aware of the extraordinary way we waste the gift of words. We use them to protect our insecurities and we cast them carelessly around our every encounter. Twisted and emptied of meaning, we litter our lives with them. Then, when we really need words to communicate, to love and to understand, we wonder that they are so hard to find.[4]

David discovered the value of words, as he withdrew for an extended period of silence. This chapter then, will need to be seen in close connection with the next, where we shall look at hearing without words.

EXERCISE

Find one of your favourite stories in the Gospels about Jesus. Spend a few moments reading through the story and try to imagine the scene. Ask God to bless your imagination, as you think about the people who appear in this story. What do they look like? What do their voices sound like? Imagine this first-century Palestinian scene with all the sounds, sights and smells that go with it. Now imagine yourself in this story.

Become one of the characters and see how it feels to be there. Then, as God leads, let the story develop for you. Make it into a meeting between you and Jesus, and listen to him.

Chapter 4

Hearing without Words

For as long as I can remember I have been busy.
I suppose there must have been a time earlier in
my life when, during long summer holidays, I would
awake in the morning and wonder how I would spend
the coming day, or days, or even weeks. But now
most of my life is to do with getting somewhere
quickly, ticking off items on my 'urgent things to
do' list, meeting deadlines and generally covering
as much ground as possible in the shortest space
of time. Of course this speaks of all sorts of things.
On the positive side, it speaks of creativity, of the
gift of work, of energy and drive; but on the negative
side it speaks of poor discipline, loss of control, and
stress. It probably also speaks of an inner need to
find acceptance and meaning through doing rather
than being, and this is the more sinister pressure.

Sanctified sauntering

In the very hot summer of 1976, I spent a week at
Ashburnham Place in Sussex with a group of Christians, on a house party. I remember it clearly. They
were days of sunshine and warmth, of becoming
still and opening up. The main speaker was Colin
Urquhart, who was then Vicar of St.Hugh's, Lewsey.
In his opening talk he made one simple statement

which has troubled me ever since. He said, 'You never hear of Jesus running anywhere.' Jesus was fit and healthy and quite able to run, but he was never driven to running. We would have wanted him to run on occasions. If I had been Jairus, I would have wanted him to run to my daughter to heal her. Martha wanted Jesus to run to the dying Lazarus. There were emergencies and deadlines in Jesus' day, but he was a man at peace, a God who came to walk in this world, not to start a race.

At this conference I stopped running and decided to walk, and even to sit and wait. But I was troubled, because somehow I knew that the drive within me to engage in unnecessary running was powerful. Nonetheless I resolved to do less running. I was beginning to discover the astonishing richness of silence. With Gerard Manley Hopkins, I was eager to pray

> Elected Silence, sing to me
> And beat upon my whorlèd ear
> Pipe me to pastures still and be
> The music that I care to hear.[1]

I was beginning to love this 'music', and resolved to become better acquainted with its melodies. My resolution did not last long. That autumn I moved to St. John's College, Nottingham, to complete my training for the ministry. I loved my time at College, but it wasn't long before the running had started up. It seemed to me that one of the main aims of College life was to cram as much learning and activity into one term as is humanly possible, and I soon found myself running down corridors to lectures, cycling fast to parish placements, and generally spending most of my time out of breath. Once a term there was a Quiet Day. A day when College stopped. A day of stillness. A day when nobody ran. It was here that I learned that not only did I want times of stillness, but I was someone who *needed* such times. They were essential to my physical, emotional and spiritual wellbeing. I looked forward to these days as lifelines, and they always ended too soon.

There is of course nothing intrinsically wrong with running. I know a part of me was made to run. We were made to run for joy, for health, to express exuberance and to experience speed. Only a few days ago, I went to my children's sports day, and saw my seven-year-old son sprinting in the running race, and watched his delighted face as he was first to the finishing line. But the running we so often do is not of our choice. It is to do with an internal race that was never set by God. The problem with this kind of running is that it dulls our senses. Those who run without pausing cease to be aware of their surroundings. Their eyes are inevitably fixed on the goal ahead, and therefore they cannot be aware of the world they are running past.

Some of course continue this race as an internal event, even forgetting quite what they are running for. They are in a race at work, and return home still internally racing, and family and friends and Jesus are left on the sidelines watching them race to some imaginary finish. This is when it all gets really sad and the running destroys not only the runner but those around him. It also means that we fail to make creative contact with the world we rush past. R.S. Thomas expresses it beautifully in his poem, *The Bright Field* which begins:

I have seen the sun break through
to illuminate a small field

for a while, and gone my way
and forgotten it. But that was the pearl
of great price, the one field that had
the treasure in it. I realize now
that I must give all that I have
to possess it . . .[2]

I am aware that often I have missed this pearl of
great price, this field of hidden treasure because I
have not been sufficiently alert. I suppose what we
are looking for is some kind of sanctified sauntering,
whereby we are content to journey in a way that is
not obsessed with the destination and is able to rest
in the travelling. This does not devalue the destination, rather it is to do with affirming the journey.
We need therefore to look at ways of developing
this ability to become aware not just of the end of
the journey, but also of all that is going on around
us while we travel.

Training in the Quiet Place

My present work with Anglican Renewal Ministries
inevitably means that I spend much of my time
involved in charismatic renewal. I love my work, and
whilst I am an enthusiast for charismatic renewal
I am also willing to be a critic of it. I see it as
part of my job. As I look out over that part of the
church which would reckon itself to be charismatic
or 'in renewal', I see a very busy group of people,
who nonetheless long for quietness and stillness.
The common caricature of the charismatic is one
who is noisy, extravert, handwaving, chorus singing

and generally rather shallow and not in touch with the real world. The history of renewal has given some ground for that view and it is perhaps a sad reflection on charismatic renewal that few observers would immediately associate it with stillness. And yet the longing is there. We are those who seem to have a need for some major project, some great target, and we would feel terribly insecure if we simply said, 'We are actually planning nothing this year.' It would seem to speak of failure. There is some logic in this, because many churches have seen the drying up of all spiritual life precisely because the leadership has been vague and directionless. But the problem with grandiose targets and projects is that we can become obsessed with the end, losing that sense of journeying-awareness.

Three times a year I meet with a support group of friends. We have one thing in common, and that is we all have a Christian ministry which takes us travelling around the country. This support group is a great security for me, and is a safe place to share our struggles and searchings as well as our strengths and joys. I went to this support group at the time when I was struggling with this problem of noise and busyness, and the need for quiet. I talked about all of this in the group, and they prayed for me and supported me. One of the group is Stewart Henderson, a Liverpudlian poet. Being with Stewart has reawakened my love for poetry. I never saw myself as a poet, but I did write a bit some years ago, but this particular stream had more or less dried up. However, after the prayer and contact with my poet friend, I woke up the next morning with a sonnet. Somehow during those hours of sleep, healing had been going on within me, and by the morning it had settled in the form of a poem:

A Sonnet for Charismatic

Last night I dreamed of a world
Without the ceaseless buzz of charismatic noise.
Someone decided to turn it off for a while.
The world noticed little difference
Except that fewer people were running
There were less hunted and haunted faces
And some bookshops closed down.
Stillness came upon Charismatic
And much dreaded nothingness.
It was a terrifying darkness of too much light
The fear of nowhere to go
The tempting insecurity of no longer being
  left behind.
And all this for one loving embrace
One tender moment for Beauty to kiss the beast.

Within this experience, there was for me that moment in which Christ had come to me in all his beauty, and chosen to embrace me in all my beastliness. This inevitably brings transformation and renewal.

If, as individuals and churches, we are to avoid the headlong rush into greater rushing, then we must learn about sanctified sauntering, and we must learn how to stop, to allow the beauty of Christ to draw close to us. A day of quiet set aside is ideal for this. I realise that for some people this is very difficult. If you have young children, or if this involves taking out a day that would normally be a holiday or a precious Saturday, then there are difficulties. But we dare not give up too easily! We need to ask God to show us when and how a Quiet Day might be possible. Even if it is only an afternoon or an evening, it will be better than nothing.

I make it a personal discipline to take one day out every four to six weeks as a Quiet Day. I spend a day at a nearby Convent. Usually there are many bits of work which beg to come too, and there is the usual pre-retreat discipline of telling them that this is no place for work!

When I arrive at the Convent I am usually still in running mode. I am still in the frame of mind which is trying to work out how much I can cram into this one short day. Perhaps I could read a complete book! Perhaps I could master the latest technique in prayer! Or maybe I could even have a good long session of spiritual warfare – anything to 'make good use of the time'. So usually my day starts with owning up to all of this, and slowing down and surrendering to God. During this time I find I want to get to know God again. It is a precious time of friendship. I like to natter to God about what has been going on, and allowing the things that are particularly concerning me to rise to the surface. I don't usually hear God speaking much to me during the first few hours. At some point I will go out for a walk, because for me walking helps me to pray. I have known times of joy on these walks as I feel thrilled with God or his world, and I have also known them to be times when I have cried out in anguish to him, desperately begging him to speak to me about something with which I am wrestling. To be honest I have also had a fair number of walks which have simply been walks and I haven't thought of anything particularly spiritually profound. But even this gives me space, and therefore is very valuable. In fact I would rather walk one hour enjoying the countryside and appreciating the space, than spending the time straining to achieve some spiritual goal that I had set myself. The walk is always an important time

We must calmly shed all noise in the name of the new leaves

of my day. Perhaps it is something to do with the physical journeying which helps me to make contact with where I am on my journey through life.

One of the great things on a Quiet Day is the opportunity you get for silence. The Convent I visit has its mealtimes in silence. I used to find this terribly uncomfortable and would take a book in to read as I never knew where to look! The problem with this is that it is very difficult keeping a paperback book open on the table when you have a knife in one hand and fork in the other! But now I am used to the silent meal, and I feel quite at home. Here is a model of being in community at a meal, yet having the freedom to refrain from words. The Russian poet Yevgeny Yevtushenko has written a poem entitled *Autumn* in which he compares the outward season with the inward autumn that needs to go on within us. There are two verses of this poem that I especially value and often come back to:

> Insight is the child of silence.
> No matter if we make no tumult:
> We must calmly shed all noise
> in the name of the new leaves.
>
> Something, certainly, has happened:
> Only on silence I rely
> Where the leaves, piling on each other,
> Are silently becoming soil.[3]

In the silence within my Quiet Day, there is the possibility of shedding my noise, and allowing new leaves to form, new insights to be born.

So my Quiet Day contains walking, praying, reading, Bible study and silence. Usually before it is time to end, I will have some sense of what God is wanting to say to me, and my relationship is in some measure restored. People use retreats and Quiet Days in many and various creative ways, and there are a number of useful books around for guidance.[4]

However we use the Quiet Day, it is a training place in awareness. Here you give yourself some space in which to learn how to listen to God, and to yourself and to God's world, and what you learn here, will affect how you live in the normal working day.

Awareness and alertness in everyday life

When we become a son or daughter of God by new birth in the Spirit, we begin a relationship with a Father who loves us. I have two daughters and one son and I enjoy a special relationship with each of them. They freely talk to me, often all at the same time, and it is part of my role as a father to listen to them, not only to what they are saying, but also to what they are not saying, to what they are feeling and to how they are experiencing life. I have learned to understand their spoken language and their unspoken language. In turn, they have learned to listen to me, and again they are learning to listen not only to my words, but my unspoken messages and feelings. Through our many conversations, we know each other well. They give me the wonderful gift of understanding what the world looks like from the vantage point of a child. In turn, I can tell them what the world looks like from my point of view.

Not long ago I was able to purchase a video camera which has been the source of a great deal of fun and amusement in our home. During the first week of its life in our family, I went around the house taking lots of film. My eldest daughter Joanna remarked, 'So that's what our home looks like to you.' For the first time she was able to understand what our home looked like for someone who is 6'1" tall. It looks really very different to how she sees it. There are pictures and shelves and decorations which she has never seen because she is only 3'1" tall. I in turn have asked her to film the home from her point of view, and I have discovered things about our house and garden that I had not seen before. For example, I had never realised how close children are to flowers and plants, to their scents and beauty.

There is a simple parable here. God desires to get to know us so that we can begin to see the world from his point of view, and he desires to experience our world from our point of view. We carry so many unnecesary burdens because we have failed to see our world from God's viewpoint. Just as it is important for me to understand my children's view of the world so it is important that they learn to appreciate and understand mine. There are times when they need someone to look over the walls to ensure there are no monsters there, or to inspect the tops of cupboards to check them for lost books and toys. The children found my height particularly useful when we once visited a maze. I could peep over the hedges and find the way through. A parent's vantage point of life gives a child security and makes the world a safer place. Children of God need to be in touch with their Father in heaven, who is a God of infinite greatness, so that we can find security in a world that can often be a bewildering maze.

A two-way communication with my children is an essential part of our family life. It would be curious if I said to my children, 'I only want you to talk with me for twenty minutes a day before breakfast and for one hour on Sundays. During such times you will talk to me and read the book I have written, but I will not talk to you. During the rest of the day it would be nice if from time to time we could think of each other, but there is no need for us to talk together.' Yet this is how it is for many in their relationship to their Father in heaven. A twenty minute 'quiet-time' and church on Sunday is the only chance God gets of getting a word in, and even then there is often the assumption that all the talking is done by the child, not by the Father.

As children of our Father then, we need to set our

minds to the very likely possibility that God will want to speak to us at any time of the day or night. The question is, are we alert to his voice? Modern western people view their lives rather like large department stores. Bits of my life are given to different departments. There is the work-department, the family-department, the God-department, and so on. God is allowed to be generally around and doing things in the God-department which has within it other sub-departments such as my quiet-time, church, fellowship group and meeting with Christians. But it comes as a shock to some to find out that our God is a God of incarnation, who actually has invaded all departments of life and who is just as likely to be found in the shopping-in-the-Co-op-department, as he is in the church-compartment. It still disturbs some today to know that Jesus was as much at ease in a pub as he was in the synagogue. We somehow imagine that he was there under suffrance, standing at the bar looking condemningly at all who came up to order a glass of wine. Actually he wasn't talking about the evils of alcohol at all. He was talking about the evils of religious hypocrisy.

Jesus demonstrated that our God is a God who likes to be involved in normal life, not just in the religious-department. So how do we hear God in the normal bustle of everyday life, in the pubs as well as the synagogues, in all the departments of my life? How can I learn to listen to his view of the world? The answer is not to do with learning techniques, but it is to do with who you are. I expect someone somewhere has produced a book entitled something like, *Seven Infallible Ways To Hear God Whilst Doing The Dishes*. We have had so many *How To* books produced in recent years, and no doubt some started reading this book in the hopes that at last you would be given some secret recipe for hearing God more successfully! Well, I am sorry to disappoint you, but I believe the truth is not to do with learning new techniques. It is not to do with doing or achieving. It is about being.

My children did not have to learn how to hear me. They heard and understood me long before they understood words. Even as babes they would watch my face, hear the tone of my voice, enjoy the sounds of laughter. Even in their mother's womb they could hear our voices and feel our presence, and understand basic messages. It is all to do with intuition and love. A child has an inbuilt instinct which is like a well-tuned radar system. They listen when there are no words. Watch any baby in one of those baby bouncer lie-back cradles. I remember talking to my children when they were at that stage. I would lean over and grin and chat, and they would giggle and gurgle back, their faces full of meaning, even though they had absolutely no clue what my words meant. As they grow older they learn to use language. They, and we, become more sophisticated as we make use of language. But still this intuitive channel is there, operational and useful. In some cases this channel is so well attuned that it can communicate across distances. This is often the case with twins. And here we meet a problem, because our occult-hazard-warning buzzer goes off warning us that we are into the dangerous waters of telepathy. It is true, occultists of various kinds have abused this instinct and developed telepathy in a way that it becomes a destructive power. But is it any worse than words being used in a destructive way? How quick we are in churches to write of such instincts as evil, when we freely use harsh words of criticism to one another. We need to move away from that departmental way of thinking which says that things are more evil or more godly simply because they are supernatural.

This intuitive ability for communication between parent and child is God-given and is good. Children learn to listen through words, but non-verbal communication still exists usually at a subconscious level, as body language, tone of voice, facial expression etc. all combine to give the overall message. I once heard it said that only seven per cent of the total message is communicated through the words. All this has something to say about how we listen to God.

Many of us struggle to listen to God because we are working only on the rational level. We are expecting to hear words put into well-constructed sentences, with good grammar and of fine literary merit. You often hear opponents of the gift of prophecy complaining about how the prophecy is invalid because the Almighty would never address us in such poor English. But all this misses the point. The point is that much of God's communication to us happens through the channel of intuition, and few would claim to be beyond infancy in their journey of learning to listen to God. Generally we should not expect to hear and understand literal words from God.

The problem with intuition is that it lies in the unconscious realm of our lives, and for many this is a dark and suspicious realm that no Christian should be seen entering into. Yet the Spirit of God can be found here, for this too was created by God in the image of God. It is actually the home of faith. Christopher Bryant writes in *The River Within*:

Faith has been called a kind of knowledge, an intuitive awareness of the unseen. Intuition has been defined as the perception by way of the unconscious. To know by intuition is to know without being able to say how you know. This quality of faith adds conviction to bare belief. 'Faith makes us certain of realities we do not see' (Heb. 11:1).[5]

Hearing God, and child-like faith are very closely bound-up. Anyone who has tried to hear God, will know that faith plays a large part in it all. We not only have to learn to open that channel of intuition in which we hear God communicating to us, but we also have to develop faith to believe it is him communicating and to walk out in it. Abraham not only heard God, but he believed him and he acted on what he had heard.

The story of Jesus and the child in Matthew 18:1–14 tells us quite a lot about this. Jesus takes a little child. (The Greek word is *paidion*, a word used for very little children who had not mastered the art of speaking.) Here Jesus takes the little pre-verbal child who is probably around one year old, and he puts him in the middle of his disciples. In so many words Jesus says to them, 'If you are looking for a model for how I want you to live in the Kingdom of God, here you have it.' He gives immense value to children and gives a terrible warning to those who would spiritually abuse them. In verse 10 we have the summary, 'See that you do not look down on one of these little ones.' 2000 years on and we still have not fully grasped this. It not only speaks of the high value of children, but it also speaks of Jesus' affirmation of the gifts of the child. One such gift is that intuitive ability to hear at all levels and to have faith.

If we are to hear God then, we will need to become

as a child again. We will need to start opening up channels that we closed off long ago, and for some of us this may even involve a measure of inner healing. We have failed to hear God because we have made it all too sophisticated, too western and too rational. As we start to become as little children again, we start to become the kind of people who will be aware and alert to our God who is communicating to us. And he is a God who will communicate at any time in any place.

So how does this intuitive level of hearing work in practice? The intuitive is to do with that part of the brain which is creative, which handles emotion, which speaks in pictures, which dreams, which sees visions. These are the areas that the Protestant church has in the past closed off so effectively. It was launched in the power of the word. It was offended by symbols; it smashed statues, icons and stained-glass windows in its attempts to return to the purity of the word, and yet the word is full of windows, of icons and of symbols. This was all in reaction to misuse. But there was once a church in this land that had word and picture in a creative balance. It was a church that existed long before the Catholic/Protestant divide. We need now to spend a few moments with this church.

The eye of the eagle

The early Celtic church in this country was the first genuine expression of British Christianity (as opposed to an imported European Christianity which came with the Romans). One of the first great Celtic saints was Ninian who evangelised Scotland at the

Hearing God and child-like faith are closely bound up

end of the fourth century. From then on the Celtic church grew apace. Its heroes were great figures like Patrick, David, Brigid, Aidan, Hilda and Cuthbert. Their expression of Christianity was one that was wonderfully earthed as well as being gloriously spiritual. For them there was no question of pushing God off to various religious compartments. He was active and speaking everywhere. The Celtic church was a visionary church that had learned to hear and see the things of God in all places. They were at home with words and teaching and they were at home with dreams and visions. They understood the rational and the intuitive, and sanctified both in evangelism and ministry. They have so much to teach us about hearing God. Great missionary endeavours came about through hearing the voice of God. Indeed if they had failed to hear God, there would have been no evangelising of our nation at that time.

The Celtic church loved the image of the eagle. Canon David Adam, Vicar of the Holy Island of Lindisfarne writes:

They prayed that their eyes might be opened, that all their senses might be made alert to that which was invisible. They prayed that they might have the eagle's eye to see Him who comes at all times. They sought to discover Him in the garden like Mary Magdalene and to be able to say, 'I have seen the Lord'. Like the disciples in the Upper Room, they shared the joy of His presence in their home, and received His peace. They expected to encounter Him when they were fishing and on the seashore, and they would be sure He shared a meal with them. Time and again they would express their love for Him like Peter and desire to follow Him forever like the Beloved Disciple. They would say in their own words, 'We beheld his glory.' They soared to the heights of awareness and saw deeper than many peoples, for they sought to see with the eye of the eagle.[6]

The Celts loved to make all kinds of situations into meetings with the risen Lord. In the same way we are invited to meet with the risen Lord in all our comings and goings. We too, are invited to have the eyes of the eagle, so that through natural things we may see the things of God and hear his voice. These Celts loved creation, not least because it was through the creation that they heard God. Mark Stibbe, in the theological supplement of *Anglicans for Renewal* writes:

Given that the Holy Spirit is at work in the creative processes of our physical world, we should cultivate the ability to listen to God within nature. This is not to say that nature and God are one and the same. It is rather to say that God's creation can be appreciated as a sacrament, as an outward sign of God's invisible gracious presence. Christian poets, novelists and artists have always understood this.[7]

He goes on to quote C.S. Lewis:

All ground is holy and every bush (could we but see it) a Burning Bush.[8]

How many ordinary bushes have we walked past which could have been for us a burning bush? How many times have we trodden on ordinary soil, which could have been for us holy ground and a moment of meeting with God? How many fields have we driven past, that may have contained treasure? God longs to speak to his children. He longs to break out of the little compartments we place him in. He longs to re-open that channel of intuition and speak to his children and hear them speaking to him. And this is the God of the Trinity: the Father desires to speak to us, for he is our Father who like any parent wants to have a meaningful relationship with his children; the Son wants to speak to us because he is a friend, who like any good friend wants to speak and listen; the Spirit wants to speak to us, for he is the 'Go-Between God', the messenger dove who carries the word of God as life to the world. God as Father, Son and Holy Spirit seeks to communicate with us, and often this will be through the created order around us. We are to develop the eagle eye – the eye that sees the risen Jesus in the creation around us, and causes us to meet with him.

Let's summarise where we have got to: If we are to hear God, then we will need to make space and spend time in sanctified sauntering, rather than becoming obsessed with the finishing post. To help us do this we may well need to develop a discipline of taking a regular Quiet Day, a place to pause and have space in which to learn to hear God speaking to us. But God wants to communicate with us at all times, not just on our Quiet Days, and in prayer times. We will therefore need to learn to be open at all times. As children, before we learned to talk we learned to communicate through intuitive channels, and it is through these channels that we are likely to hear God speaking to us. Like the ancient Celts, we need to develop the eye of the eagle, to see unseen things, and to find the risen Jesus in the world around us.

EXERCISES

1) If you do not already plan to have a Quiet Day, take some time to think about whether you could plan one.

2) Reflect on your own life: has it become too busy? How can you develop some sanctified sauntering in your lifestyle?

3) Think back to the time in your life when you were a baby, unable to communicate through words. Imagine how it felt to communicate non-verbally and through the world of intuition.

4) Spend time in being open to God. Try and listen to his non-verbal communication. What are his feelings towards you? What kind of messages do you sense he is communicating to you?

5) Ask God to give you the eye of the eagle, that your spiritual vision may be sharpened. Then take an opportunity to walk down your street, in your garden or in the country and be open to the risen Jesus meeting you.

Chapter 5

Hearing and the Holy Spirit

Not so long ago, my wife, Julia, and I were invited to the Anglican Chaplaincy in Brussels to lead a Saturday Conference. It was a training day for those doing the *Saints Alive!* course. During the afternoon session, I spoke about the gifts of the Holy Spirit, and in particular I focused on those gifts identified by St. Paul in 1 Corinthians 12:7–11. Of the nine gifts mentioned in this list, five of them are to do with listening: the message of wisdom, the word of knowledge, prophecy, discerning of spirits and the interpretation of tongues. Having taught about this, I then instructed the gathering to move into groups. In these groups we would learn together to listen to God, trusting the Holy Spirit to send his gifts among us. I joined one small group, settled down in the silence, opening myself to hear God. The church hall settled into quietness with everyone straining to catch a word, or a picture, or to be directed to a Bible passage. Try as I might I could not hear a thing, but odd pictures of a butcher's shop kept invading my mind. As if this wasn't silly enough, my mind zoomed-in to a close-up of a collection of very tempting looking sausages which were well displayed in the front window. 'Surely,' I thought to myself, 'God has not brought me all this way to bring a message about sausages!' No, I was into idle daydreams, and this could not be the voice of God.

Eventually the time of silence ended and it was

time to share in the groups what we sensed we had heard. I went round my small group. Not one person had heard a thing! Just as I was about to launch into my well-prepared speech about how God does not always want to speak in this kind of way and we should not feel a failure if we don't hear him, the lady next to me suddenly said, 'All I could think of was the fact that I had forgotten to take the sausages out of the freezer that we were meant to have for supper tonight.' This sent me into something of a panic! What was going on? Here I was in Brussels entering into an apparently quite ridiculous piece of investigative research on sausages and their spiritual implication! I owned up in the group that I too had been preoccupied with sausages during the time of silence, which of course amused the group.

But then we started to talk about this together. We realised that God had indeed spoken, but he had spoken in a riddle, just in the way that Jesus used to teach his disciples. Eventually we discerned that God was saying something to the church through these pictures. This was a church in which the Holy Spirit was clearly at work, and the gifts of the Spirit had been exercised. But there was a sense in which the church had put the gifts into the freezer for storage, rather than taking them out and using them. God wanted to breathe his warm Spirit of love on the church, releasing the gifts for evangelism and ministry.

Pentecost and dreams

This kind of experience is very common to those who are involved with charismatic renewal. Charismatics have always been impressed by the immediacy of God who wants to come and live and move among us by his power. But such immediacy is of course available to all God's children, and one of the channels that the Spirit delights to use is the intuitive channel that we looked at in the last chapter. This is the channel used by dreams and visions. The prophet Joel, himself a man who had learned to hear God, predicted a widespread release of the Holy Spirit through which others would hear God:

And afterwards,
I will pour out my Spirit on all people.
Your sons and daughters will prophesy,
   your old men will dream dreams,
   your young men will see visions.
Even on my servants, both men and women,
   I will pour out my Spirit in those days.
(Joel 2:28,29)

The apostle Peter makes full use of this Scripture in his Pentecost sermon. The outpouring of the Spirit on the group of disciples as recorded by Luke in Acts 2 is in direct fulfilment of this prophecy. The widespread release of the Spirit will involve a release of prophecy which will often be expressed in dreams and visions. From earliest times it was expected that prophetic insight would be delivered through dreams and visions. God tells Moses, Aaron and Miriam that 'When a prophet of the Lord is among you, I reveal myself to him in visions, I speak to him in dreams.' (Num. 12:6)

The evangelical wing of the church has always been a little suspicious of this intuitive channel. They are on the whole more comfortable with the secure world of the word, rather than the dark waters of the subconscious. And yet dreams and visions figure prominently in the Bible. Russ Parker in his book, *Healing Dreams* writes:

> Immediately you open the pages of the Bible and look for the subject of dreams there is a startling contrast with today's popular scepticism of their usefulness. Dreams are respected; they are listened to and generally there is a response to their message. Far from being a topic of fringe interest, they are dealt with in some detail and taken very seriously. There are in the Bible over 130 references to dreams and almost 100 to visions, the bulk of them in the Old Testament.[1]

Herman Riffel, another Christian writer on dreams goes as far as to say that if you add together all the direct references to dreams and visions together with the stories surrounding them and the prophecies that issued out of them, then we would find that about one third of the entire Bible is related to them.[2]

It comes as no surprise then, to discover that the coming of Jesus into this world was heralded by an extraordinary activity of the Holy Spirit communicating through dreams and visions. Mary, Joseph, Zechariah and the Wise Men all hear God through this medium.[3] The outpouring of the Spirit at the birth of the church signals the beginning of a community of faith that is regularly directed by the Spirit through dreams and visions. Here we have a vibrant church which regularly recognises the guiding activity of the Holy Spirit in dreams and visions. We will look at two examples of where a dream or vision changed the direction of the church:

1) Acts 10:9ff. Here we have the well-known

story of a hungry Peter on a rooftop in Joppa. From his own hunger pains there develops a visionary experience of seeing a sheet being lowered from the sky with animals that he deemed unclean. In this vision he is warned not to call common what God has cleansed. The result of this dream is that the evangelistic efforts of the church are now directed towards Gentiles as well as Jews. If Peter had not been open to this vision, the consequences would have been very serious.

2) Acts 16:6ff. Paul is on his second missionary journey and finding that the Holy Spirit is closing off one region after another. The enthusiastic Paul must have been frustrated at this and was longing for clear guidance. He rested at Troas, then during the night Paul had a vision of a man in Macedonia who was calling them to come over and help. Paul has no doubt that this is the guidance of God, and Luke tells us that, 'After Paul had seen the vision, we got ready at once to leave for Macedonia, concluding that God had called us to preach the gospel to them'. This was their natural conclusion – God had spoken through a vision.

The Bible ends with one spectacular vision given to John on the island of Patmos. This must be the most extraordinary, frightening, wonderful and profound vision ever given to anyone. Through the picture-language of the vision, individual churches are spoken to, and the vast cosmic themes of life, death, good, evil, the end of this age and eternity are all covered. If such serious things are communicated by God through the picture-language of vision, we dare not dismiss this medium as one of God's means of speaking to us.

From time to time in my travels I come across people who have been clearly spoken to by God in a vision. One January I led a conference at St. Michael's Church, Eastbourne. This was a church with a High Church tradition which has been undergoing an exciting renewal. John Harrington, the Vicar, has been there a number of years, but life has not always been easy for him as he has pioneered renewal. However he has remained steadfast even through difficult times, not least because of a vision he was given in 1986.

One night he dreamed that he was awoken by the sound of banging, which was coming from the direction of the church. He went out of his house, up to the church which had been covered in scaffolding, and saw, on this scaffolding, a number of men working hard. As he approached, the church was bathed in a golden light which caused John to feel utterly elated. He enquired of one of the workmen what they were doing. A man working near him spoke to him in a voice that sounded like lapping water. He informed John that 'the young man' had instructed them to work and surround the church with this protection. The 'young man' was as a brilliant light above the church radiating light and warmth. In this dream John was warned that he and the church would enter a time of testing, but to fear not, for God had surrounded the church with his protection. With this the dream came to an end and John woke up. The feelings of the dream were still powerfully with him and he could hear a sound like the banging which was at the start of the dream. He went down to investigate and found that the back door and the garden gate to the church were wide open, despite the fact that John had shut and bolted them both before going to bed. Whether it was a dream or a vision I do not know, but either way, John had an experience which ministered deeply to him, and was a powerful way of hearing God.[4]

In the complex and wonderful book of Job, there is a useful reference to dreams by the young counsellor Elihu:

> Why do you complain to him [God]
>   that he answers none of man's words?
> For God does speak – now one way, now
>   another – though man may not perceive it.
> In a dream, in a vision of the night,
>   when deep sleep falls on men
>   as they slumber in their beds
>
> (Job 33:13–15)

The young Elihu here shows real insight into the confusing world of hearing God. He has understood that there is no set way for God to speak – he uses a whole variety of ways, not least the language within dreams. Because we have ignored for so long this important part of our lives, we have a lot of catching up to do in terms of understanding the language of dreams. Dreams and visions usually are in the form of parables, and as with all parables, they will often be like puzzles and we will probably need the help of others to work out what they are saying. Sensitivity and carefulness will be required and it is most important not to leap to hasty conclusions.

A few months before our third child, Lucie, was born, a good friend in our church, someone who was good at hearing God, awoke one day from a powerful dream about Julia giving birth to the child three weeks early. Our first two children had come late, and those last days of waiting in 'extra time' were exhausting and depressing. The thought of a child coming early therefore greatly encouraged us.

*How in the cacophany of voices that makes up me am I
going to distinguish the voice of the Holy Spirit?*

Influenced to some extent by wishful thinking, we hastily assumed that this was a warning dream telling us to be alert to this early birth. As it turned out Lucie was late like the other two, and hopes of an early end to a long pregnancy were dashed! We had to learn through this that dreams nearly always speak to our own situations rather than someone else's. This friend acted out of kindness and love for us, but it now seems that the dream was more likely to be speaking in parable to some area of her own life rather than God warning us. But that experience has not closed us to the very real possibility that God speaks through dreams.

Not long ago the team who are involved in the work of Anglican Renewal Ministries were agonising over a particular connection we had with a business that worked for us in the production of our magazine and courses. This was under serious financial pressure, but because we liked the people, we wanted to stay with them, even though we were starting to come under financial pressure ourselves because of this. We had to make a decision, to stay with this arrangement or to pull out. Then, one day, one of our prayer partners, a good friend from our old parish, phoned to say that she had had a dream about us being on a train that was about to go over a precipice. People were trying to encourage us to stay on, but she knew she must warn us to jump off. She had no idea of the situation we were in. This indeed was a warning dream from God. The dream confirmed our feelings, and we separated ourselves from that particular business. Not long after that the business collapsed and it is very likely we might have gone the same way had we remained closely connected. It was a sad time as we saw good friends suffer, but we were grateful to God for warning us.

As we learn to respect our dreams and the dreams of others, so we will become open to the possibility that important messages may be conveyed through them. It may be a communication from my subconscious to myself, warning me or guiding me about some matter. On the other hand it may well be a dream inspired by the Holy Spirit and thus a means through which the beloved Go-Between communicates God's message to me.[5]

Pentecost and promptings

Whilst dreams and visions from God may still seem rare, it is not at all uncommon to hear people speaking of having *promptings* from God to do things. This is a very important part of hearing God and one fraught with difficulties! This is all to do with developing an intuitive ability to pick up the leading of the Holy Spirit. In the Acts of the Apostles we find a community of people who really became very accomplished in this. I like the story of Philip and the Ethiopian eunuch in Acts 8:26–40. We know that Philip was a bold and powerful missionary. He had been in Samaria where he had been engaged in evangelism, healing and deliverance. A lovely testimony to Philip's ministry is the short verse (Acts 8:8), 'So there was great joy in the city'. Philip was a joy-bringer, one of the most important ministries in the church. An angel appears to him (v.26) and gives him a rather strange instruction – to move away from the fertile fields of Samaria, and go down to the desert road.

On arriving at the appointed spot, Philip waits for further instructions. This time there are no angels, but we read, 'The Spirit told Philip, "Go to that chariot and stay near it."' Now the question is *how* did the Holy Spirit tell him? Did a voice come from heaven? Was there writing on the sand? Did God use a passing stranger who directed Philip in the direction of the Ethiopian chariot? The only likely explanation is that Philip experienced an inner prompting, a kind of instinctive hunch, an intuitive knowledge that this was the chariot to go to. And with faith Philip goes and he has got it right. I suspect (and hope!) that Philip also had a number of times when he got the hunch wrong, certainly in his early days. But he had learned from Jesus this skill of listening to the Spirit's promptings, and the Ethiopian eunuch for one was eternally grateful that he had.

The Holy Spirit still desires to communicate in this way. In the last ten years, thanks largely to the ministry of John Wimber we have seen the gift of the word of knowledge restored. Thousands of people in this country have been helped into healing, because someone at a service or a meeting has been prompted with a hunch and has been bold enough to share it. From my experience of training people in the healing ministry in my parish in Kidderminster, it was usually the more intuitive people who were open to this. I used to love the looks of astonishment on peoples faces as they risked sharing a word of knowledge and found it to be accurate.

This is certainly not the only way, and neither is it in any way superior to any of the Spirit's other ways of communicating, but it is nonetheless a very useful and practical way. There is no set of techniques for mastering the art of being proficient in Holy Spirit promptings, it is not to do with doing, but is to do with being. And it is to do with being with God. If we are desiring to deepen our walk with God, to be open to his communication night and day, and not just for a twenty minutes prayer-time once a day, then we will inevitably be learning about these promptings.

To catch these promptings we will need to learn to practise the presence of God in all that we do. This is where the Celtic church was so strong. There was no compartmentalisation in their Christianity. Every event during the day was an opportunity to include God. The Celts took to praying and listening at all kinds of moments of the day and connecting what they were doing in the material with the spiritual. Hence lighting a fire in the morning was not just about starting a fire to keep the house warm. It was much more:

> As I light this fire, Lord
> I bend my knee and lay myself before you.
> Kindle in my heart a flame of love
> Love to warm my home and my dear ones
> Love to cheer my neighbours and this
>   community . . .[6]

It is this kind of weaving together of our world and the world of the Spirit that will open us to his promptings. In this way any event that takes place, any scene we may see, any conversation or meeting that occurs, may well be the setting for a prompting of the Spirit. Not long ago I was on Holy Island in Northumbria. It was a blustery, cool but sunny day and I was struggling. I was struggling to find the Lord and to hear his voice. I had come away on this retreat in the midst of a busy time at work and here I was far from home and away from work, and I really was not sure why I was here, and I felt weary. I expressed my struggle by striding across the sand-dunes and eventually reached the sea. Here I walked along the beach and found a group of young people coming towards me. 'I don't want to see any people,' I complained to the Lord, 'Is there nowhere I can go to get alone?' On I grumbled as they got closer, and then I felt the prompting which simply said, 'One of them will ask you a question, and it will be an important one. Take note of the question and of your answer.' It was not spoken out as a voice, it was just an impression which I have translated into English. Sure enough one of the young people bounced up to me and asked, 'How far is it to the caves?' I did not even know there were caves in the region so I rather feebly replied, 'Sorry, I don't know, I've not been there.'

On I walked back to the sand-dunes, and then I reflected on the conversation. Suddenly it dawned on me. During the summer I had become gripped by the discovery that the dove that descended on Jesus at his baptism was probably the rock dove, which is a bird whose natural habitat is in wild and rocky places, and who makes its nest in dark recesses and caves. This is a lovely picture of the Holy Spirit who delights to come into the darkened caves of our lives and of this world and bring his life. The reference to caves led me back to this theme that had been developing in my heart for some time. As I returned to this theme I found more and more clues to help me in my present struggle. I knew God had spoken to me. It had started with a prompting, and it set me on a trail to peace. At the end of the walk I was restored.

The voices within

The really difficult thing about all this, is to distinguish the voice of the Spirit from all the other voices within us. There are voices of hope and voices of fear; there are voices of pain from the past and voices of assurance; there are voices of guilt and voices of freedom. There are complicated negative 'life scripts' which rise up like curses over our lives deafening us to life-giving messages. How in the cacophany of voices that makes up me, am I going to distinguish the voice of the Holy Spirit?

The answer is that I must learn to listen to many of them so that I can identify them. Some of them are so deep-rooted that I will probably never hear them, and would only need to if it were required for my wholeness. But others are a little nearer the surface.

Dietrich Bonhoeffer, during his captivity in solitary confinement, wrote a poem which has long been one of my favourites. It is called *Who Am I?* In this poem he struggles with this very question – who is he? Is he a confident Christian facing difficulties with courage and a smile, or is he a frightened bird in a cage with longings and dreads? He is actually both. Both are part of the authentic Dietrich. Both are voices within him that must be heard. But it is the punchline of this poem which gives us a starting point:

> Who am I? They mock me, these lonely questions of mine.
> Whoever I am, thou knowest O Lord, I am thine.[7]

To dig and delve into our inner selves without some undergirding is dangerous. Any inner exploration

91

requires care and stability. Our stability comes from the knowledge that God knows us. He knows us intimately. He knows the voices that confidently rise up, and he knows the voices that sit in shadows; he knows the voices that speak of going out on adventures, and he knows the voices of weariness that seek to lie down and rest. For our God is a God who has searched us out and known us, and before a word is on our tongues, he knows it completely (Psalm 139). Yes, he knows the many voices within us and he can identify them. When I know I am known that well and loved, I am free to explore.

Through dreams and daydreams, through counselling and through prayer I will get to know myself better. By silencing all censoring voices of condemnation, I can allow my voices to be heard. Some will need to be affirmed and given space; some will reveal wounds which will need healing; some will speak of deep yearnings and longings that will be turned into prayers; some will speak of strengths I did not know I possess; some will speak of weakness which will remain so that the power of God may have room to move in my life. It will always be hard to hear the voice of God when I am hiding behind a veneer of Christian respectability. George Herbert was a man who greatly loved God, and he could hear him. He was not afraid of sharing his feelings with God, and on one occasion when he felt angry and trapped, he wrote a poem called *The Collar*. This poem begins dramatically:

> I struck the board and cry'd, No more.
>> I will abroad.
> What? shall I ever sigh and pine?

As the poem proceeds we get the full force of his anger and frustration, and it builds to its final crescendo,

> But as I rav'd and grew more fierce and wilde
>> At every word,
> Me thoughts I heard one calling, *Child*:
>> And I reply'd, *My Lord*.[8]

As I get to know myself and my voices within, then I will start to be able to distinguish which is the voice of the Spirit.

The groaning of the Spirit

We have seen then that the Holy Spirit, in many and various ways, helps us to hear God. He sanctifies and uses that intuitive channel and opens to us dreams and visions and inner promptings. He helps us identify and listen to those other voices that speak within us, and he comes with healing. The activity of the Holy Spirit in communicating God's word to us is of course so vast that several books could be written on the subject, but there is one other area that I would like to cover before we close this chapter.

Once a year, I and the other staff at Anglican Renewal Ministries, meet with our Advisory group who guide and counsel us. At one of our meetings, Bishop Simon Barrington-Ward of Coventry led a Bible study on Romans 8:18–27. He spoke about the groaning of the Spirit and compared it to the groaning of Jesus in the Garden of Gethsemane. Here in this passage, we have an insight into that work of the Spirit that communicates to us the groaning of God. For when the Spirit comes to us, he comes to woo us to the heart of God. And here we not only start to hear words of knowledge to do with things like painful knees or heart problems, but we are taken into the more profound things of God. Here we are permitted to get so close to God that the Spirit himself, the Spirit who was upon Jesus in the Garden of Gethsemane, intercedes in us. He knows the mind of God, and he intercedes for the saints in accordance with God's will. This passage must be dwelt on and dwelt in, because it is all about the Holy Spirit who perfectly hears God, and who moves in us. As the Spirit ushers us into this holy place we hear the groans of God, and they are groans for his creation. Here is the place of true charismatic renewal, and any renewal that bypasses this groaning will produce malformed children. Graham Kendrick has caught something of this groaning in his hymn of confession:

> Who can sound the depths of sorrow
> In the father heart of God
> For the children we've rejected
> For the lives so deeply scarred?
> And each light that we've extinguished
> Has brought darkness to this land,
> Upon our nation, upon our nation
> Have mercy, Lord.[9]

There is something terrible about all of this. Hearing God can be a terrible experience because we begin to make contact with the *feelings* of God, and we begin to hear Gethsemane-groanings and Golgotha-cries of anguish. I sense that the Spirit of God is calling us afresh to draw near to the sacred heart of God that has been broken for the world.

The Spirit will use all sorts of ways to enable

us to hear the heart of God. The church where I served in Kidderminster was situated on a small council estate. This was in many ways an estate that represented a forgotten part of Britain. It did not hit the headlines by having riots, and it did not qualify for being an urban priority area. Very few from this community came to church, not least, I suspect, because they had felt betrayed and abandoned by the church many years ago. One night I caught a glimpse of the heart of God for this community. The church adjoined a hall which was much used by the estate. This particular night there was a sale which promised wonderful bargains. Many from the estate had gone down to the hall in the hopes of catching a cheap video or microwave or some other such thing. In the event they were conned, and many of them lost large amounts of money. The conmen escaped and the place was in uproar. I, as the Vicar, was called in to subdue the crowd, which was not a role I relished. I arrived at the hall feeling responsible because it had taken place on our premises. I looked round at the angry, betrayed faces. Once again the hope of winning had been denied them. I stood there silent as they made their protests, and I felt the heart of Jesus going out to them. They were like sheep without a shepherd. That night the Spirit of God groaned within me as I came in contact with God's feelings for this community, and thereafter my predominant attitude to this estate was one of compassion.

But we need to remember that these groanings are birth pangs, not death pangs. Labour pains are fierce, but they herald life, and so, paradoxically, while we feel the feelings of God for this tortured world, we also experience profound hope that one day our Lord Jesus will return to give birth to a new age of the Spirit, a new creation, a new heaven and a new earth.

EXERCISES:

1. *Start recording your dreams and ask God to speak to you through them. You don't have to have a degree in Psychology to understand your dreams! Ask the Holy Spirit to bless your dream-life, and become expectant that God might speak to you through this.*

2. *Make a decision to become more open to the promptings of the Spirit. As you go about your daily work, become aware of the presence of God. Turn daily routines into prayer and be alert to God speaking to you through them.*

3. *Ask God to reveal to you something about the voices within you. Are there any particularly strong ones that you need to hear and acknowledge? See if you can identify some of them.*

4. *Meditate on this verse from Romans:*

> We do not know what we ought to pray for, but the Spirit himself intercedes for us with groans that words cannot express.
>
> (Rom. 8:26)

5. *Become aware of the heart of God for this world and for the community where you live. As you become aware of his heart, invite the Spirit to stir you to prayer.*

Chapter 6

Hearing God Together

I arrived at St. John's College, Nottingham in the autumn of 1976 and found I had been placed in a small tutorial group which met for worship most weekday mornings. The tutor in charge of my group was Graham Dow, who is now Bishop of Willesden. I immediately warmed to Graham and soon found him to be a good friend and wise counsellor. These were the days when St. John's College was pioneering charismatic experience in College life. It was not uncommon to witness speaking in tongues or prophecy[1] in the College midweek Communion service, we sang songs from the *Fisherfolk* (a group from America who at the time took a lead in renewal music) and a number of the College staff spoke openly about their own charismatic experience. Having come from a University theological faculty where the staff viewed with grave suspicion any immediate operation of a gift of the Spirit, it was something of a culture shock to be in another theological environment where there was a high sense of expectation about God doing things, and exciting things at that, in the here and now. Graham was one of the members of staff who spoke boldly, yet gently, about his charismatic experience, and he encouraged our small tutorial group to be open to gifts of the Holy Spirit.

I remember one day coming to the group, and Graham saying, 'This week we are going to look at prophecy together. Paul says in 1 Corinthians

14 that he wants all to prophesy and recommends to the Corinthians that they should all prophesy in turn.[2] This means it must be possible for us all to prophesy, so when you come tomorrow morning, please be prepared to do so.' Graham has always had that knack of asking the impossible of us in the most matter of fact kind of way! The next morning came and we duly prophesied, and it was one of the most moving group meetings I have been to. We had got to know one another well as a group, and it was hard to know what was human and what was divine, but certainly everyone there had a thought, a word, a picture for others in the group, and we each felt greatly encouraged. For some in the group it was the introduction to this particular gift of the Spirit. For myself, I had been acquainted with it for a little while.

I first became aware of charismatic gifts when I was eighteen years old. In my last term at school, I, with Gerald a good friend from the School Christian Union, visited a nearby Pentecostal church. The services at this small Elim church were rather different to the kind of services held in the lofty school chapel where we normally worshipped God. In the Elim church we heard people speaking in tongues and also reciting things which sounded to me like bits of the Authorised Version of the Old Testament, and yet I could not place them. I had no understanding then of the gift of prophecy. Having been prayed for by the Elim pastor for the pentecostal experience of *Baptism in the Spirit*, Gerald and I started to speak in tongues. We had a strong desire to meet regularly together to pray, and the chaplain, who was decidedly cool about our new-found charismatic experience, very graciously allowed us to meet regularly in the chapel vestry for prayer. For him, it probably kept the thing contained in a safe place; for us, it was a nice secluded room and we could pray in tongues to our hearts' content without anyone interrupting us! We were like young children with a new toy and we enjoyed all the exuberance that a new-found spiritual experience gives. During one of these happy prayer-times, I had a strong sense that Jesus wished to speak to us. Not only did he wish to speak to us, but he actually wanted to speak through *me*! So, with some trepidation I said, 'I think Jesus wants to speak through me, and he wants to say this . . .' I can't actually remember what was said, but I remember a sense of shock, and a sense of anxiety, a fear that I had in some way been blasphemous. Yet both Gerald and I sensed God's presence with us. The school chaplain was doubtful about this experience, but the Elim pastor was more helpful. In a letter to me he wrote, 'You don't need to worry about that – God has given you the gift of prophecy. I should welcome it!' Later we went to see him and he gave very useful guidelines for future use of the gift.

The gift of prophecy

In this chapter we want to explore how we can hear God together and how we can encourage that gift of the Spirit called *prophecy*. The gift of prophecy must be one of the most difficult gifts to learn and to manage. It is difficult because it is personal and requires discipline. It is difficult because prophecies and prophets can be easily misunderstood. It is difficult because it feels a fearsome thing to bring words from Almighty God. It is difficult because many of us have had bad experiences of rather arrogant people bringing a *word from God* when quite clearly they are bringing us something more from their own agenda than God's. It is difficult because prophets traditionally have been rejected. So, when all is said and done, it feels a lot easier to ignore it and go on to simpler things!

And yet, it is a gift of the Spirit that has traditionally been highly valued by the early church. As we have seen earlier, the great promise of the Holy Spirit given in Joel 2 anticipates a widespread release of prophetic activity, and the early church picks this up and runs with it. St. Paul gave great value to the gift:

> Follow the way of love and eagerly desire spiritual gifts, especially the gift of prophecy ... everyone who prophesies speaks to men for their strengthening, encouragement and comfort.
>
> (1 Cor 14:1,3)

This is a tremendously important verse. If I were Paul, speaking to the wild charismatics of Corinth, I don't think I would risk saying, 'eagerly desire the spiritual gifts'! I have a feeling I would want to stop them being so spiritual and tell them to learn how to clean floors and wash the dishes. But Paul has a great heart for the church, and when he sees the church going wrong, he does not try to put the brakes on or try distraction tactics, he draws it back on to the right track with love and clear teaching. So here, he sees a charismatic church in some confusion. He sees men and women who seem to have a particular preoccupation with speaking in tongues. Now I understand this. When I first spoke in tongues it was a wonderful release, and when I am in a meeting and we sing in tongues together there is often a glorious sense of the presence of God among us. Like Peter, I would like to try and 'build tents' at this point, and enshrine the experience so that I can stay there and thoroughly enjoy myself. But Paul says, *'Follow the way of love'*, and here's the catch. When we come to church the idea is not to drift off into individualistic flights of spiritual pleasure, but it is to love and serve the church family who are present with us. The Corinthians are eager to have spiritual gifts, and Paul does not mind this at all, but he stresses, 'Since you are eager to have spiritual gifts, *try to excel in gifts that build up the church'* (v.12)

Paul is keen that people coming to church should come with a clear expectation that God wants to speak, and he will speak through many people in the church. There may be one or two people who are particularly gifted in this way, and they are called *prophets* (v.29), but notice what he says in v.26, 'When you come together, *everyone* has a hymn, or a word of instruction, a revelation, a tongue or an interpretation. All of these must be done for the strengthening of the church.' Paul clearly expects lots of people to be hearing God for messages that will strengthen the church.

Now interestingly, this use of prophecy is not for judgement, but for strengthening, encouragement and comfort. It is used here in a pastoral way. God loves his church, and he has given these gifts through which he can express his love and build us up. But how many churches today honestly have been open enough to encourage people to hear God in this way?

It was not just the New Testament church which gave a high value to these prophetic gifts. In the early centuries of church life, prophecy was greatly valued. It has often played an important part in spiritual revivals of these times. Two revivals that particularly move me are the revival in Egypt, and the revival which first spread Christianity to this land.

The desert fathers in Egypt
Following the conversion of the Roman Emperor Constantine, and the subsequent end of persecution in the early fourth century, materialism and nominalism entered the life of the church and in many places it became very worldly. But this gave rise to a spiritual revival which gave birth to monasticism. Thousands of men and women went into the desert either alone or in communities. Here prophecy was given a high value, and many would come from towns and cities to these lonely places, and when they had found a holy man or woman, they would ask him or her for 'a word', and the holy person would give them a prophetic word. They lived in expectation of God speaking his word through one another.

The following story of Abba Moses and Zachary is typical. The term 'Abba' was given to those desert fathers who were outstanding in terms of spiritual maturity and wisdom. Moses, prior to being a Christian, was apparently a brigand. But once converted, his life was transformed and in time he was viewed as one with considerable spiritual authority. People would come to him for advice, but Moses was far from being a proud man, and he was always alert to listening to God, even if God should speak to him through one much more junior than he. The story of his conversation with a young disciple called Zachary illustrates this. Moses went to Zachary one day and said:

'Tell me what I must do.' At these words, the

disciple threw himself at the old man's feet and said, 'You are asking that from me, Father?' The old man replied, 'Believe me, Zachary my son, I saw the Holy Spirit come down upon you and since then I must consult you.'³

Abba Moses was a man who had learned to see the activity of the Spirit upon people. He could see the Spirit moving on Zachary in such a way that Zachary would speak prophetically to him. This kind of experience was very much at the heart of this revival.

The Celtic church
In the early Celtic church, prophecy was given a high place. Indeed many men and women became leaders and evangelists as a result of people prophesying over them. The seventh-century Northumbrian saint, Cuthbert, was one of the greatest of the Celtic saints, and at the age of eight he was challenged by a child who was 'no more than three years old' who upbraided him for playing when he should be preparing himself for the ministry to which God was calling him. This young infant called him 'a priest and bishop', a prophetic insight into what Cuthbert was to become.⁴ The Celts had no difficulty in believing the promise in Joel 2 that 'your sons and your daughters will prophesy'. When as a young man, Cuthbert entered the monastery at Melrose, he became especially close to the abbot, a man called Boisil who must have been a lovely and gentle man. At one time both Boisil and Cuthbert caught a fatal plague. Cuthbert was healed, but for Boisil it was the means through which God was calling him home. Boisil knew this, and chose to

*Thousands of men and women went into the desert either
alone or in communities*

spend the last week of his life with Cuthbert. The
Venerable Bede tells us that during this week, they
read together John's gospel which they finished
quickly, 'because they dealt not with the profound
arguments but with the simple things of "the faith
which worketh by love"'. Bede tells us that during
this extraordinary week Boisil 'is believed to have
unfolded all Cuthbert's future . . . He was a prophet
and a very holy man'.[5]

But despite these lessons from history, we are
still slow to learn about this vital gift for church
life. A Vineyard Pastor from Colorado called James
Ryle wrote a book in 1992 with the unlikely title
of *A Hippo in the Garden*. The title is explained
on the back cover: '"Friends, I have a word from
the Lord for you . . .". Have you ever cringed at such

a greeting? You are not alone! The words sound as frightening and incongruous as a hippopotamus crashing around in someone's carefully ordered garden.' In this book, James Ryle attempts to reassure those who have been put off by ham-fisted attempts by well-meaning people to prophesy. In his chapter on the prophetic ministry, he writes,

> Apostles, prophets, evangelists, pastors and teachers: according to Scripture, these are the ministries which Jesus Christ gave to His Church to equip her for service ... That is how the Lord gave them, and that is how they are to be received. Yet, today, only three out of these five 'gifts' are widely accepted throughout the Body of Christ (i.e. evangelist, pastor and teacher). The remaining two are held at arm's length and viewed with awkward suspicion by many within the mainstream of evangelical Christianity.[6]

Traditionally, evangelicals have been very wary of any claimants to the titles *Apostle* or *Prophet*, believing that the biblical writers are the true apostles and prophets. Because of the status of the hierarchy in the Catholic church, there is reluctance to see prophetic ministry develop among lay people. Therefore in traditional Catholic and evangelical spirituality there has not been the experience of prophecy such as I have described above. But prophecy has always been a subject of interest in pentecostal and charismatic spirituality and in recent years there has been a renewed interest among charismatics in the prophetic gifts and ministry and I am personally in no doubt this is at the initiation of the Holy Spirit who wants to restore the prophetic ministry to its rightful place in the church. But because we have had centuries of generally ignoring it in the church, we have got a lot of catching up and learning to do. So how do we start?

The learning group

In my College Tutorial Group, it was not difficult for me to attempt a prophetic word. I had been doing it for a number of years, and although for others in the group it was quite new, I noticed how the environment of the group enabled people to prophesy, and from that time on I have always believed that the small group is the best place for learning. Such a group that wants to learn about prophecy will need to develop a good level of trust, because anyone learning to hear God and to speak out what he has said, is bound to make mistakes, but in a small group with a high level of trust there is no need to fear this.

I have quite often led groups, where I have encouraged them to be still and listen, usually for about five minutes, depending on how comfortable people are with silence. Before this time of listening, I will explain about the gift of prophecy, which I interpret fairly broadly as including words, pictures, impressions, feelings, memories of incidents or dreams – whatever the Spirit chooses to bring to mind. The important thing is to be open and to allow the Spirit to put something in your mind without your immediately censoring it and declaring it unfit for group use! It is the group's responsibility to 'weigh' the prophetic word.[7] Just prior to the silence, I will invite the Holy Spirit to come with gifts of revelation.

I really do believe that the Spirit is terribly practical and does not mind in the least bit if we 'practice'. Although we are handling holy things and we need to retain our sense of reverence and respect, we are nonetheless children who are learning, and learning is creative and fun. So it does not surprise me when the Holy Spirit puts unlikely or even funny things into people's minds. I sometimes wonder how it must feel to God, when he gathers a group of his people and over coffee they light up with chatter and laughter, but as soon as they get to the 'spiritual part' of the meeting they put on their solemn faces and look earnest. I think I should feel somehow rather left out.

I pray then for the Spirit to come and speak to us, through us, and I might use the opening verse from that great hymn of invocation:

> Come Holy Ghost, our souls inspire
> And lighten with celestial fire;
> Thou the anointing Spirit art,
> Who dost thy sevenfold gifts impart.

In the silence we listen, and for most of us it is a mixture of daydreaming thoughts, embarrassing feelings (someone's stomach nearly always chooses to rumble at this point), and little snatches of God speaking. The more we practise, the more we learn which is which. After the silence, I might ask the group to break into pairs and then each talk together about what they heard and sensed. This breaks the ice, ice which is to do with fear of looking foolish. After a time of sharing in pairs, we then share back as a group. It may be that some very clear things are shared, but as we saw in Chapter 2, it is quite likely that God will be speaking to us in the form of parables and puzzles. In one such group I was leading a little while ago, I was given a picture in my mind of a small girl standing by the sea shore. She was afraid because some trauma had happened in the sea. I mentioned this to the group, and one person immediately 'owned' this picture as hers. As a small girl she had become terrified of water, because her aunt had drowned in the sea while out swimming. We prayed for her, for God to heal the memory and to help her feel safe in water. I saw her the next week and she was quite exuberant. She felt changed within after this group ministry. She decided to take her daughters to the swimming pool. Not only was she happy for them to go in, but she also joined them and thoroughly enjoyed it! In small groups like this, faith levels can rise, confidence grows, and the wild extremes can be checked.

My colleague at work, Alan Price, a Church Army Captain, works with children, and he is finding that many children are very responsive in such small groups. Children enjoy listening to God and are very open to receiving pictures, which they then draw or paint and discuss. On many occasions these drawings and paintings have been means through which God has spoken to his people.

Hearing God for individuals

Many churches nowadays are developing healing teams and groups who are available for listening, counselling and prayer ministry. It is in the area of counselling and inner healing, that prophetic insight can be a powerful key. It was Jesus' prophetic insight into the Samaritan woman's marriage problems that led to her healing and salvation. Some years ago, I was helping on a healing and personal growth week at a retreat house. I led a group of about a dozen people; each morning, before the group met, I would wait on God and ask him to speak to me and show me anything that would help anyone in the group. One day I felt him speak to me about someone who I will call James. I heard in my mind a text from Deuteronomy which turned out to be an obscure verse which included the words, 'You will be cursed when you come in and cursed when you go out' (Deut. 28:19). This made no sense, so I did not pursue it, but felt it would probably have relevance some time that day.

In the group, James started to share a problem he was having with claustrophobia, and as a minister in a growing congregation this was becoming increasingly a problem. Alongside this he was also developing a fear of people shouting, and as he was in a Pentecostal church this was a handicap! After listening to him, as a group we prayed, and the Holy Spirit took this man back in his memory right to that moment in his life when he was born. But as he was reliving his birth, ready to emerge into the world, he felt panic and dread. He could hear his father shouting, words he could not understand, but he knew they were hostile words that spoke of rejection. He wanted to go back into the privacy and safety of the womb, but couldn't. But he couldn't face being born. The words from Deuteronomy came back to my mind, 'You will be cursed when you come in and cursed when you go out'. This precisely summarised James' terrible dilemma. But we knew God was in the business of releasing people from curses and giving his blessing. To share this verse with James brought great release. For him it was a sign that God knew what it had been like for him all those years ago. God had listened to his pain then, and that knowledge alone brought him great healing. With the gentleness of the Spirit, and free of the curses that had ensnared his life, he was able to be born and not hear the tirades of an angry earthly father, but feel the love of his Father in heaven who blessed and welcomed him. James testified later that this had produced a profound healing in his life, and he is now quite at home in pentecostal crowds!

I am personally fairly uncomfortable with the idea that anyone at any time is likely to get a word from the Lord for an unsuspecting friend. I have seen much damage done by heavy-handed people launching into poor victims who are told intimate details of their life. But in pastoral situations, it is much more likely that God will speak specifically to individuals. It is my experience that when praying for someone I will feel a kind of surge of the Spirit which ignites my praying, and I find myself praying more and more precisely for that person, until I am not sure whether I am praying or prophesying. This is not surprising, because as I start to pray in the Spirit, so it is quite likely that I will start to see in the Spirit. Those who feel called to use prophetic insight in their ministry should be aware that the insight could well be given while they are in the flow of intercessory prayer.

There is another area here that we need to consider. In the last couple of years, it has become more common at charismatic meetings to see individual prophecy practised from the platform. In the course of 1990, charismatic renewal was introduced to a new name – Paul Cain. He had become a good friend of John Wimber, and many in Britain so love and trust John Wimber that any friend of John's is a friend of ours. We heard reports of Paul's remarkable prophetic ministry, and in the summer of 1990, John Wimber brought Paul Cain and other prophets from Kansas City to London for a meeting. Holy Trinity, Brompton was filled with people eager to find out what all this was about. On occasions at these meetings Paul Cain would speak and give out some remarkable individual prophecies. A word frequently used was 'awesome' as Paul Cain gave out names of people whom he had never met nor heard of, but had 'seen in the Spirit' during the course of his lengthy prayer-time. Also at this meeting, various people were introduced to the prophets and given personal prophecies to encourage them.

These men were referred to as 'The Kansas City Prophets', and they returned again in the autumn to a series of meetings which became rather confused with promises of revival, or part revival. The charismatic world was suddenly thrown into confusion, and many remain confused and sceptical. I suspect it will take us some time to understand and weigh-up all of this, and I would expect that the kind of public prophetic ministry of the sort that Paul Cain practised will not be one given widely in the church. But it has brought to our attention the impact of God speaking directly into people's lives. We are still infants in this field, and as infants we have the fatal tendency to either jump on bandwagons or over-react and miss something important that God has to say.

I know I learned something important through all of this. As I went to these meetings, I discovered within me a longing to receive a 'personal prophecy' from one of these men (preferably at one of the private interviews that were being arranged, rather than in the public auditorium which seemed terribly embarrassing!). It was actually quite a difficult time for me, a time when we were seeking God about the future of Anglican Renewal Ministries. Should we move our base from Knaresborough? If so to where? Should we take on an extra member of staff? There were lots of unanswered questions, but I failed to get an interview with any of the prophets so I had to go away without my prophecy! I soon realised that this desire to get a red-hot prophecy was me trying to short-cut again. The Lord was dealing with me in his own way and in his own time. God did speak to us through 'usual means' and made his will perfectly clear. Added to that, eighteen months later I was speaking at a Roman Catholic Renewal day-conference at Ampleforth, and at the end of the day a Catholic woman humbly took me to one side and with an endearing sense of awkwardness prophesied to me. It deeply moved me not least because this spontaneous prophecy came in the form of beautifully constructed poetry, and I learned from this the need to be open to God speaking to me through whom he will, when he will.

Hearing God for the church

As we have seen earlier in this book, Jesus taught his disciples the importance of listening to the voice of God and hearing his word. One of these disciples was John to whom Jesus gave the nickname *Boanerges*, meaning *Son of Thunder*. This Son of Thunder must have been a wonderful character. The reference to thunder surely indicates a man of noise and power. Together with his brother James, he was furious when certain Samaritans rejected Jesus on his journey to Jerusalem. 'Lord, do you want us to call fire down from heaven to destroy them?' they ask, hoping no doubt that Jesus would be thrilled with their zeal. Instead, they are the ones who receive the rebuke and their thunder is stilled. But during their three-year apprenticeship with Jesus they learn to surrender their thunder to Jesus. That is not to say that the thunder is dispersed. Rather it is sanctified, and we see John emerging as a man of tenderness and power. His tenderness is seen at the foot of the cross as Jesus entrusts his most precious relative, his mother, to John. The thunder in John speaks of great depth, and according to early Christian tradition, it is while he is a prisoner of persecution on the island of Patmos, that the sanctified thunder is released in a most extraordinary and wonderful way as he is sufficiently open to God to receive arguably the most powerful vision ever to be received by man. His listening to God, on this lonely island, carried him to the very portals of heaven and time, where he could see things revealed which had hitherto remained closed and hidden. The fruit of his hearing and seeing is recorded in the book of Revelation, a book so mysterious that much of its meaning is hard to grasp. But it is a book that must be appreciated through the faculty of intuition. We must listen to the feelings in it, and allow ourselves to see the visions, and hear the sounds. It is a drama which must, so to speak, be seen on the big stage, and loses its effect if it is studied by nit-picking students who want to use it for forming doctrines.

The Bible ends therefore with a book of revelation. This is significant. The word of God ends with an invitation to see and hear through dreams and visions. The book ends with glimpses of heaven, and words of glorious hope, in the opening verses of the final chapter. Jesus himself addresses the apostle, and assures John, 'I, Jesus, have sent my angel to give you this testimony for the churches'

(Rev. 22:16). This book is speaking to churches, not just to individuals. And it begins by specifically naming seven churches which receive clear prophetic warnings and encouragements. The difficulty with the book of Revelation is working out quite what is literal and what is allegorical. We must be honest about this and acknowledge that much of our interpretation has to be speculative. But let's consider for a moment the prophecies to the seven churches.

The first thing I notice is the basic principle, that Jesus has specific things to say to specific churches. In other words he has things to say to individual churches. At the end of every prophecy, we have the words, *'He who has an ear, let him hear what the Spirit says to the churches'*. It seems to me that this is a tremendously important statement, especially as it is repeated seven times. It is making clear that the Holy Spirit has a special relationship with churches in communicating the message of Jesus. It also implies that it is perfectly possible not to have ears to hear, that it is quite possible to be deaf to the voice of the Spirit – and this should concern us.

So, just as Jesus will speak to individuals, he also wants to speak to local churches. Just as he wants to speak specifics to individuals in the form of personal prophecies, so he wishes to speak specifics to churches, and the reference at the start of each prophecy, *'to the angel of the church of . . .'* suggests this same personal approach. We need now to identify some general areas that he is likely to speak into. There are four that I find are common:

1) The spiritual condition of a church
This is the case for the Laodicean church – its condition is lukewarmness. While I was working

as a Team Vicar in Kidderminster, there was a ten-month period in 1985/6 in which I was acting-Rector for St. George's church during an interregnum there. I appreciated very much the opportunity to draw closer to this church, which had been originally the mother church of the parish. St. George's was a traditional church, with high ceiling, robed choir and much more formality about it than the other two churches in the team. During my early days in Kidderminster there was the suggestion from some of the more enthusiastic members of the congregations of the other churches, that St. George's was dying, and that the life was in the two younger churches. I must admit that I never had any sympathy with this view, as I had seen St. George's grow and it had a good foundation for further growth. When I was asked to become acting Rector, I remember enquiring of the Lord about St. George's and its spiritual condition. God answered me through a dream.

I dreamed that I was with a group of friends, and we were in an old building. We came across some tombs, and on one of the tombstones we could clearly read the writing which told us that this was the grave of a young girl who lived in the sixteenth century. We were inquisitive about this girl, and we decided to lift the tombstone to investigate further. Inside we saw the body of the little girl, perfectly preserved. In fact she was not just preserved – she was alive! One of the friends with me was a doctor, who diagnosed that this girl was in a state of coma, and indeed as we looked at her she 'came round', got up and started to dance round the building. There was something very endearing about this child, but she was, at first, very ill at ease. The doctor commented that this was very likely because she would take

115

her time to get used to twentieth-century life. Sure enough, in time, this girl did get used to her new time, and she settled down and was very loveable.

It was a very vivid dream, and it did not take me long to understand it. The girl represented St. George's church. The dates on the tombstone spoke of Cranmer's prayer book, and although St. George's church was not prayer book, it had a very traditional feel about it. The message in the dream was that the church was not to be viewed as dead, but that it had known a time of dormancy. But now it was waking up, and as she woke up, she would struggle for a while to re-orientate herself in the late twentieth century. I believe that God spoke to me through this dream. It gave me a great love for the church, the same love I experienced for the little girl in the dream. I no longer had any doubts that St. George's was in a process of waking up spiritually, and now six years on from that dream, there can be no doubt that it is a church that is awake and growing.

2) Direction for the future

It is not uncommon for churches to get to 'stuck places', where it becomes hard to see where to go next. In the summer of 1988, I was seeking the Lord for direction for St. Chad's, the church of which I was Vicar. We had seen a lot of growth. We had built an extension, and we had done some mission work. We had developed a healing ministry, and we were starting to develop a wider ministry to the Diocese in terms of sharing renewal. But I was very keen that we would not get into the trap of jumping on to the next thing, just because it seemed a good idea, or because it was the kind of thing other churches were doing. This concern was expressed by the Church

Council, and it was decided we should have a day away together.

I very much looked forward to this time away, and prayed that God would give me a word, or some sense of direction for the day. As it got nearer, a number of the Council asked me what the agenda was going to be. It would have been tempting to have panicked into forming one just to give us a sense of security. But I could discern nothing. A few days before the meeting, I started to panic. 'Lord, I can't call a dozen people away from their families on a Saturday just to sit around and admire the scenery. Please tell me what you want us to do!'

I was then given a sense of quiet, and I felt God say to me, 'Open your Bible, but keep your eyes closed.' I opened it and thumbed through the pages until I had a clear sense that I had landed on the page that God wanted to show me. Here at last would be a text, a Bible story, a prophecy, something that would give us direction for the day. 'Open your eyes and look at the page and you will see what I want you to take to the meeting.' With a great sense of anticipation I opened my eyes, and looked down. At first I was not sure whether to laugh or cry: Staring up at me was a completely blank sheet of paper. I had opened it at the page in my Bible that separates the two Testaments! I soon realised that this was God's word to me and I could almost hear him chuckling. All we had to take with us to this day was a blank page on which God could write. We had done enough talking, writing, projecting, speculating. Now was the time to listen.

On the Saturday of our meeting, I broke the news – that I had come with nothing! I sensed some discomfort in the meeting and noticed those rather kindly yet puzzled looks that people give to their clergy sometimes, which says something like, 'Is there anything we can do to help – you are obviously under some pressure?' However, not daunted, I led the Council into a time of stillness and asked everyone to open their minds and hearts to God, as blank pages upon which God could write a message to us, for direction for the church.

I shall never forget the next hour or so, in which every member of the Council shared words, pictures, impressions etc. which communicated to us God's heart for the church. By the end of the day, we felt we had heard God clearly. As a church we had become too noisy, too busy, and we had to slow down and listen to him. As a sign of our commitment to this, we gave the first week of the year as a time to listen to God. Whenever there was a standard church meeting, we changed it into a prayer meeting, and we held prayer meetings each night of the week. We would follow the same principle – start in silence with blank pages, then let God speak to us. At each meeting, God did speak about a number of things in our church. Once we had heard him, we moved into intercessory prayer for those particular issues.

One of the things we found ourselves constantly led to pray for was the young people of the estate. We seemed so out of touch with them, and we felt God's heart for them. The following Sunday, we had our once-a-month Communion service at St. Chad's. With the main evening worship usually being at St. George's, these services were very small. Usually no more than about fifteen would come, and they were quiet intimate services. However, on this Sunday, in addition to the fifteen regulars, the church was suddenly invaded by a squadron of twenty young people who suddenly decided to make us a visit. They giggled and chattered in the back of the church, and I felt awkward and not a little afraid. But when we came to the intercessions, Tony a stalwart at the church and a man with a real heart for the young people, stood up and said, 'Before we go on, I think we should just thank the guests who have come tonight.' He then turned to the restless gang and told them about our prayer-week, and how God had told us to pray for them. They got the shock of their lives when they realised that they were in church because God had called them there!

3) *Healing of the church*

As we have seen, churches are like individuals. As individuals we have our own personal histories, which to a large extent determine our behaviour. In recent years, the Holy Spirit has released a lovely grace of inner healing. Inner healing often involves the healing of painful memories. Just as individuals have painful memories, so have churches. Some of these memories may be recent or they may go back centuries, just as some of the deepest hurts in our lives may go back to our earliest years. So it is, that a number of churches are researching their history and enquiring from God about their spiritual history. It is not uncommon for churches, either through research or gifts of discernment, to discover wounds from the past. Through repentance and prayer, churches can receive healing.

I know of one church, where sadly the Vicar had to leave for sexual misdemeanours. The Vicar who came after him became quickly aware of the hurt and the pain left in the church as a result of this trauma. I was with him at a conference during his early days in his parish, and in a small prayer-group one person who had been carefully listening to God for the situation, had a very clear impression that this man should lead the church in a weekend of prayer, fasting, and repentance for the past sins. The weekend was duly held, and I was very impressed with the way this leader offered repentance on behalf of the previous incumbent. With this as a foundation, teaching was given on the Sunday on marriage and relationships.

One interesting touch follows this story. A little girl came to church with her mother that Sunday. Later in the week she said to her mother, 'Mummy, I like going to church now. The witches have gone from the windows.' With the insight of a child, she had discerned sin and evil in the church which had been expelled at that important weekend.

4) Spiritual warfare

Shortly before taking up my appointment as Director of Anglican Renewal Ministries, I was taking a Quiet Day in Malvern, praying about the work. During this time I felt God speaking to me about various issues in the life of the church, one of which was to do with spiritual warfare. I had never had any difficulty in believing in the reality of spiritual warfare, but neither had I ever given the subject a lot of attention. However, in the course of this Quiet Day, there was a moment when I felt I heard the sound of battle – I could hear a strange mixture of ancient and modern weapons, clashing swords, and powerful guns. There was a strong feeling of sadness in this, and I believe I heard God's voice which said, 'The battle is fierce and many of my churches are in the midst of battle, and some are dying because they have no understanding of the warfare they are in.'

It was this experience that led me to set up training days that we called 'Prayer Combat Days'. We held twenty such days across the country, and the main purpose of these days was to help churches become better equipped in the spiritual battle. It is still not a subject that particularly appeals to me, but I believe it is one that is vital for churches to be aware of. Spiritual warfare is not a special-interest subject for Pentecostals. It is part of the life of every baptised Christian. When I was baptised as a two-month-old baby in St. John's, Edinburgh, the Vicar held me in his arms and exhorted me to 'fight manfully under the banner of Christ against sin, the world and the devil, and to remain his faithful soldier and servant for the rest of your life'.

As I travelled round the country leading these days, I met many weary warriors who knew only too well what it meant to be involved in the spiritual warfare in their churches. As part of these training days we would have a time of silence in which we would listen to God for him to speak to us about our churches, particularly to alert us to areas of spiritual battle about which we should be praying. Frequently during these times people would have Bible verses, pictures, etc. which gave helpful insight into hitherto unseen spiritual realities in church life. This could then be prayed about, strengthening the whole church. A number of churches are becoming much more sensitive now and are giving time to listening to God about the spiritual warfare in their church, and indeed their community.

Listening and life

I have become convinced that the way for churches to move forward is to give time to listening corporately to the voice of God. It is not an easy task, and will require training and changing of long-established patterns.

In the autumn of 1991 at our National Conference, one of the key speakers was an Episcopal priest from Virginia called John Guernsey. In a moving way he told us the story of how God had dealt with him over his *workaholism*. He led him into a six-month 'detoxification' programme, in which he cleared his diary every morning to give time to worshipping God and listening to him. He would go to the church and pray in front of the altar. It was not long before others joined him, and this principle of giving time to listening to God started to percolate through to every department of church life. One lady who served on the church Council commented, 'Being on the church Council has been a three-year training in learning to hear God'. Surely, this is a church which is on the right track, where listening to God is given a high priority and is included as a regular part of church life.

EXERCISES

1. *Reflect on your church. How does it listen to God? What opportunities are there for listening to God together? Pray for your church that it would become a listening church.*

2. *If you are part of a small group, see if there are opportunities to exercise the gift of prophecy together. Take note of what has been written in this chapter – learn together, be free to make mistakes, you will probably hear a mixture of your own thoughts and God's, work with the parables and puzzles. (NB: Please don't go to your leaders*

with grandiose prophecies, especially if they are not familiar with this gift. You will not be popular, and will probably put the cause of listening to God back several years!)

3. *In your intercession for the church, give time to God to speak to you about its spiritual health and about the spiritual battle.*

Chapter 7

Discovering My Natural Way of Hearing God

We are nearing the end of our journey of exploration. In this book I have shared some of my discoveries on this journey. I have still a long way to go, and am excited at the thought of all that is yet to be discovered on this subject of hearing the sounds of God, in this busy and noisy world. But whilst I am aware of what is to come, I also have learned something about myself and my natural ways of hearing God, and it is possible and indeed essential to do this, no matter how much of a learner I may be.

I mentioned earlier in this book my friend and colleague, Alan Price, who has a lovely and special ministry amongst children. Alan is a songwriter and one of my favourites of his, has the line *'I'm a unique part of Father God's creation'*. Despite the fact that there are millions of us, we are each unique. Even in the same family there are clear differences in appearance, personality and temperament, spirituality. This uniqueness must be taken into account when listening to God, because hearing God is a *personal* engagement. It is not to do with mastering techniques, it is about getting to know God and being known by him and the communication that occurs as a result of this special relationship. Therefore depending on my personality, spirituality, background, influences etc., I will have my preferred ways of hearing God, and the vital thing is both to be

We are nearing the end of our journey of exploration

open to discovering the new, but also being content with what I know. So we each have to find a place of peace about hearing God as we are able, and not feeling under pressure to hear him as others do. We all know that heavy sense of failure that comes when we have read another thrilling paperback of super-heroes of the faith who among other things, seem somehow to have got listening to God tied up and sorted out once and for all. The problem with this is that we then belittle the ways we have learned to hear God, in the face of apparently much more effective ways of hearing him.

If we are honest, most of us are really very insecure in this department of our Christian lives. Take for example the person who has learned to hear God through opening the Bible 'at random' and discovering a verse that speaks to their situation. This kind of approach to guidance and hearing God is roundly condemned by many, ridiculed by most and would certainly be disastrous if prescribed as an acceptable way for all Christians to hear God. But the problem is, God views us all as unique, and there will be some for whom this is an excellent way of hearing God perhaps because they have a humility and lack of cynicism, and openness of faith to believe that God can speak to them in this way. But this person then moves in circles where their way of hearing God is lampooned and they are made to feel foolish and immature. They are told that there are far more mature ways of hearing God, and they should learn to put away childish things. The insecurity rises to the surface, the well-tried way is abandoned and the person is left wandering in a wilderness, searching for the word of the Lord.

We therefore need to find a place of security in all of this, so that we can be confident in our own ways of hearing God, and unafraid to experiment and explore new ways. I end this chapter then with two basic ground rules, which are important to bear in mind, if we want to grow in hearing God.

1) Knowing myself

To hear God will inevitably involve a process of learning to know myself better. My personality, temperament and spirituality will cause me to be attracted to particular ways of hearing God. If my personality is essentially introvert, then I will prefer stillness and solitude as environments in which I listen to God. If my personality is essentially extravert, then my preference will be for the group as my favoured environment in which to listen to God. Many of us have both introvert and extravert within us, but it is often the case that we have only experienced one way of hearing God, thus satisfying only one part of our personalities. An overbearing spirituality can be responsible for this. For myself, my spiritual beginnings were in evangelicalism, which was then influenced by my experience of charismatic renewal. Bible reading and the gifts of the Spirit were ways of hearing God which suited part of my personality, namely the extravert part. However, there was a frustration in my attempts to hear God, because only part of my personality was open to hearing him. When I acknowledged, that within me there was also an introvert, I opened myself to a Catholic spirituality which gave an important place to stillness, sacraments, pictures, icons, imagination etc. Discovering the introvert within me and, so to speak, welcoming him, opened new possibilities for hearing God. I know myself now, much better than I did some years ago, even though I acknowledge there is still much to discover!

2) Willingness to explore

With the security of knowing myself and knowing and trusting the ways I have learned to hear God, I can explore other ways. As the saying goes, *nothing ventured, nothing gained*. We need to have much more of a sense of adventure in our Christian lives, if we are to learn to hear God, and Christian adventure always has been and always will be, to do with faith. In *Borderlands*, David Adam writes:

> I believe that we are all called to extend our vision, our awareness, our sensitivities. Quite often we fail to 'see' because we have been unwilling to go far enough or deep enough. Quite often the statement, 'I do not believe' seems to mean, 'I am unable or unwilling to go any further'. It is amazing that so many of us think faith comes through 'natural growth' without work on our part. There is as much chance of having a strong and healthy faith without working at it, as there is to have a garden full of flowers if we leave it to nature.[1]

God has all sorts of ways of training us in faith. In my experience, he does not force this training on us. It is, generally speaking, up to us to decide how near to the edge of faith we are prepared to walk. The closing pages of this book record the story of how God led some of us to work with Anglican Renewal Ministries. It has been one long lesson of learning to hear his voice, often at difficult times. We have had to learn new ways of listening to him, as well as relying on well-tried ways. At times we seemed to hear nothing at all from heaven, and at other times we heard God's voice so clearly. The past few years has been for me a journey to new territories of faith that I had not hitherto visited. At times it felt far too near the edge, and yet I must admit I would not have done it any other way.

In the garden of Eden after that fateful moment when the man and woman succumbed to temptation, and sin entered their world, Adam and Eve became afraid of the sounds of God in their garden. Now that our world has been visited by the Word of God incarnate, we need no longer be afraid. God is calling us out from our hiding-places in which we have become dull and deaf, and wants to walk with us, healing us of our deafness and those things which have made us deaf to his voice, and leading us in the pathways of faith.

EXERCISE

1. *Spend a little time reflecting what you have learned while you have been reading this book. Spend time alert to God to see if there are particular learning points from this book that need to take root in your life.*

2. *At the end of chapter 1, you gave thought to the three 'streams' that have been referred to in this book, namely catholic, evangelical and charismatic. How do these streams now flow in your life?*

3. *Ask God to show you how you now need to explore further so that you can grow in your hearing the sounds of God.*

4. *This book ends with an appendix, which is a write up of part of my own journey of learning to*

listen to God. You may find it helpful to take an episode out of your life and write about it, paying particular attention to how God communicated with you during that time, and reflecting on how you have learned to hear him.

Appendix

A Journey Forward

I record here an account of how God led a group of us in the period July 1988 to March 1991. This was a period during which I learned a great deal about hearing God. Much of it is really very ordinary and I regret it is not filled with spectacular miracles or signs in the heavens. However, I'm not completely sorry about this, for life is mostly played out in the ordinary things, and these are the training places of faith.

In search of a vision
In July 1988 I drove back from Nottingham to Kidderminster feeling content. I had just finished teaching at a Counselling Summer School at St. John's College. We had had a good week and I had enjoyed myself. As I drove home I remember feeling pleased that I was driving back to a welcome place of settledness. I had been Team Vicar of St. Chad's Church in the parish of St. George's, Kidderminster for over six years. My five-year contract had been renewed and there were a number of challenges ahead of us as a church. In the Diocese we had formed a Diocesan Renewal Group and I felt I was starting to make a contribution to Diocesan life in this way (the other way being as an enthusiastic if

incompetent member of the Diocesan Clergy Cricket team). I loved living in Worcestershire, a county where my grandmother lived for many years. Especially I loved the Malvern hills where I would go from time to time for walks and recuperation. Driving home that night I found myself happy at the prospect of spending many years working in this Diocese, in this lovely county.

That was Friday night. On Saturday morning the phone rang as I was preparing my Sunday sermon. Someone who I hardly knew told me that Lawrence Hoyle, the current Director of Anglican Renewal Ministries was retiring due to poor health and they were looking for a replacement. This person had been awake all night with my name on their mind, and felt they should ring me to enquire whether or not I would be interested in considering the job. I said I was most flattered, but felt far too junior and suggested several names instead. However, my caller was fairly persistent, and I agreed that at the very least I would give it some thought and prayer.

My wife, Julia, and I prayed about it that evening. I was feeling so settled and I did *not* want to move. Besides, we would have to move to North Yorkshire, which was a county we hardly knew and seemed a long way away from our friends and families. It is our custom to read the readings in *Living Light* together, and that night we opened the book for the evening of 26th July. Somewhat to my horror, we found ourselves reading the words,

By faith Abraham, when called to go to a place he would later receive as his inheritance, obeyed.

I am the Lord your God, who teaches you what

As I looked at the sheer beauty and strength of these hills I became aware of a strong sense of the Spirit with me

is best for you, who directs you in the way you should go.

We live by faith, not by sight.

Get up, go away! For this is not your resting place.

This was the first of many occasions when God would speak to us through the story of Abraham, who by faith was willing to be uprooted and travel to a new land and a new calling. These verses from *Living Light* were the first of many indications from God that we should pursue this new work. Much to my surprise, during the following weeks, the close friends who I told about this all felt it was something God was calling me into. It was important for me in this listening process to ask good friends to listen to God on our behalf.

I struggled with leaving Kidderminster and Worcestershire. But I also struggled with the fact that I felt very ill-equipped for the job. Then one night I had a series of dreams. In one I was running in a race. I was younger and more junior than the other competitors. Although I lost my way on several occasions, I nonetheless did well in the race. In another dream, Julia and I were running a restaurant and thoroughly enjoying ourselves. We were having great fun, despite getting some menus confused and meals burnt! I listened to these dreams; I don't think they were God speaking to me, but I think they were voices within my subconscious having a say. They were telling me that I could run this race and in doing the new job, there would be a great deal of fun. In retrospect, both dreams have proved accurate.

In September of that year I went to meet a group of the Anglican Renewal Ministries Trustees in Oxford. As Lawrence was the founder director of the work, this was the first time the Trustees had had to appoint a new Director. A number of names had been suggested to them, and at this stage they were making informal explorations. As they did not know me well, some of them had asked to meet with me. I had now had two months to listen to God about this. As far as I could detect, he was certainly encouraging me to move forward in this direction. But this meeting with the Trustees would be an important test. And so I had a couple of hours with Teddy Saunders, David Bishop, David MacInnes, James Haig-Ferguson and Don Brewin. In my journal I wrote:

> I came away with a mixture of feelings – excitement, self-consciousness, awareness that I had been with a group of men who had been to some

deep places with God, and a sense of my own unworthiness. Also I had a strong sense that the Lord will give us a clear way forward, and that if the Lord does want us at Anglican Renewal Ministries, I won't have to struggle for it.

After the meeting I went into Greyfriars Chapel and sat in the silence for some time. I remember feeling rather depressed. At the end of the meeting, Teddy Saunders had said, 'What we are looking for is a man with a really big vision of what God wants to do in the Church of England at this time.' This was the note that was ringing in my ears as I left, and it stayed with me in that chapel. 'Yes, Lord, Teddy is absolutely right. The next Director must be a man of vision. But the problem is I do not have that vision.' I knew enough about vision to know that it was not something that could be invented. Vision is given by God, so now the ball was in God's court. If he wanted me at Anglican Renewal Ministries, he would need to give me that vision.

The Trustees felt it wise to cast the net wider as they sought for a new Director, and they advertised in the Church press. I felt much happier about this and it gave more time for thinking and praying. In November I heard that I was one of three, shortlisted for the job and I was invited to attend the interviews in early December. The day I heard I had been shortlisted, I wrote:

I still live in a tension – there is much that excites me about the job, but I also have my reserves. We don't want to leave here, I don't want to move away from the Diocese. More importantly Anglican Renewal Ministries needs a man of vision. Yet, all I can see is that the

135

witness of friends, my reading of Scripture and 'inner promptings' all suggest that I should at least go for interview.

A few days before the interview I went for a quiet retreat at the Convent at Malvern. It was very cold and snow had fallen on the tops of the ancient hills. During the afternoon I walked across these hills, calling out to God to speak to me and direct me. I would only go for this interview if he gave me a vision for the work. But nothing came. I was beginning to consider withdrawing my application.

After supper I decided to go out again for another walk, this time through the streets of Malvern. The moon beamed down on the snow-covered tops of the hills as I strode along the lanes still asking God to speak to me. As I looked at the sheer beauty and strength of these hills I became aware of a strong sense of the presence of the Spirit with me. An inner prompting said, 'Walk to the end of this road, look left and there I will show you a vision for the work.' I had nothing to lose, and besides I had no idea by this stage where I was in Malvern, so I walked on as commanded. Sure enough, the road came to an end, and I looked left. There in front of me was a sign-board, and on it a picture of a tree with ten fruits on it. Then, in a rare moment of really hearing the voice of God very clearly, I heard, 'These are the fruits that I want Anglican Renewal Ministries to bear for the church. I will show you six now, and four at a later stage.'

I started my return journey to the Convent and on this journey it was as if in my mind's eye I could see each fruit being picked from the tree and opened up in front of me. I have already written about the fruit that is spiritual warfare. The other five were

Celebration, Prayer, Worship, God's Mighty Acts and Prophecy. The last fruit was revealed during the evening service of Compline at the Convent. I have to admit, that it has not been often in my life when I have had such a clear vision or sense of God speaking to me. But it was a fairly crucial time in my life.

I felt God had given me a vision. I would share it with the Trustees at the interview. It would then be up to them to decide whether or not this was the right vision for the job. They evidently felt it was, for they offered me the job. Curiously enough, the phone call from John Gunstone offering me the job came as Julia and I were watching that wonderful episode of *Yes, Prime Minister* to do with the appointment of Bishops. The phone rang, just as there was some complaint in the story about moving north!

Taking the vision on

Not long after my appointment as Director, it became apparent that we would need an administrator to work with me. Lawrence's daughter, Jane was prepared to stay on for a short while, but we would need to find someone to replace her.

In our church there was a couple called Robert and Sue Ashman. Julia and I had got to know them and instinctively liked them from our first meeting with them. Bob was converted through the local house-church, but had moved to join our Anglican church. In due course he felt it right to become confirmed. The confirmation service was just after my appointment. Suddenly it came to mind what an excellent administrator Bob would make! This was supported not least by the fact that in recent weeks in conversations, he had casually said that he would like to leave his present job of teaching, and look for work in Christian administration. He had even said at one point that he would love to live in North Yorkshire! This was before he knew we were considering moving.

Once news of our move was out, we had Bob and Sue round for a meal and asked them what they thought about upping sticks and joining us in Knaresborough. They were excited by the idea, and on a cold January day we drove up to Knaresborough to talk with Lawrence and Margaret Hoyle about the job. Something resonated within Bob and Sue, and it was not long before they could say with confidence that God was calling them to move up to Knaresborough to work with us. This was wonderful news for us.

My last Sunday was Easter Sunday (26th March) 1989. By now Bob and Sue had put their house on the market for sale. At the time of our departure from Kidderminster it seemed that they had a firm buyer for the house, and they could start looking for a house in Knaresborough. They found one they liked, but then the sale fell through. This was the beginning of the housing slump. Had we known then that it would be nearly two years before they would find a buyer for the house, Bob would have withdrawn his offer of working for us and gone back to his old job of teaching! But as it was, we assumed this would only be a temporary set-back. God had called Bob and Sue to Knaresborough, it would therefore not be long before he would release the house and supply them and their two young children with a new home in Knaresborough. We left in April, by which time Bob had given in his notice at school, and had agreed to start work at the beginning of June.

For Julia and I and family, the early days in Knaresborough were good ones. I had a time of bereavement following the loss not only of a much-loved parish, but also of parochial ministry. I would often say to people 'I'm like a shepherd without the sheep.' It felt very strange going to church on Sunday and sitting in the pew rather than doing something from the front. But apart from this, we settled-in well. There was no doubt, this was where God wanted us and we loved living in North Yorkshire. But we got increasingly concerned about Bob and Sue's house. Not long after arriving in Knaresborough, I wrote,

> It is becoming a time of really having to hold on to God in trust. The question of Bob and Sue's house is one that we are struggling with. Humanly speaking the situation is bleak, but the Lord keeps causing me to come across Scriptures which remind me that he is trustworthy. This morning he referred me to Psalm 77. It is a psalm about crying out for help, but also remembering the deeds of the Lord – 'You are the God who performs miracles.' We need a miracle now to get this house sold.

By the end of April it was clear that with their Kidderminster house unsold, Bob would have to come and live with us during the week, going home at the weekends. This was something Sue had dreaded. She was born with partial eyesight, and depended on Bob to get her around. The thought of not having Bob around from Monday to Friday was not one she welcomed. And there were the two young children, Bethany and Jack, who needed their father. What was God doing? Had we heard him wrong about Bob coming to work as Administrator? But each time I grew desperate, God would come back to me with

almost maddening regularity. My entry for 25th May
is typical of a number at this time:

> And still God speaks and reassures. The Living
> Light readings yesterday were very powerful.
> Another Abraham verse, this time Gen.21:1,
> 'the Lord did for Sarah what he had promised',
> and other verses like, 'Trust in him at all times,
> O people . . . But God will surely come to your
> aid and take you up out of this land he prom-
> ised on oath to Abraham . . . He who promised
> is faithful'.

In May I went for a day's retreat at Parcival Hall
which is the Bradford Diocesan Retreat House, beautifully situated amid rolling hills and dales. I strode
across a nearby hill letting God have the benefit of
all my feelings about this frustrating situation. Why
should Bob and Sue have to suffer in this way? Why
could God not shift houses? And what did all these
promises about trusting him mean? I walked in the
stiff May breeze, and then had a strong sense of calm,
and the presence of God. I had already learned that
God is not put out when we let our frustrations and
feelings out before him. I felt he had heard me, and I
sensed again a quiet reassurance that he was working his purpose out, which would be different from
what I imagined. I sensed him speaking to me about
faith. We were having to learn Abraham-like trust.
Like Abraham it was easy to think of ways of forcing
the pace with God. God spoke clearly to Abraham
about having children through Sarah. When this
didn't happen, Abraham tried to do it his way with
Hagar. I had to learn to surrender to God, to let him
do it his way.

In June Bob moved in with us, leaving Sue and

*God spoke to both of us that we would move to Derby when
the leaves returned to the trees.*

the two children on their own during the week. This
was far from easy for them, but it worked, and Bob
settled into the work. By September, our church, St.
Andrew's, Starbeck, offered Bob and Sue the use
of a house it owned. This was the good news. The
bad news was that the house was virtually derelict!
However, for the sake of being together as a family
they decided to move in, which they did at the end of
October on a rather cold and gloomy day. The three
winter months in this cold and damp house are three
months that the Ashman family are keen to erase
from their minds! I found it almost impossible to
pray about the situation. Still no sale on the house in
Kidderminster, and here was this family, faithfully
following God into the unknown – and he treats them
like this! It was hard for us to listen to God during
this time, but when I did hear it was always about
trusting. For example, 22nd November:

Got worried again about Bob and Sue – again the Lord encouraged me. He put a Bible reference in my mind – Romans 4:3. Yes, I should have guessed, it's about Abraham!

At the end of the winter, the Curate at St. Andrews left to go and work in Argentina. This meant that the Curate's house became available, and in February, the Ashman family moved into a much pleasanter and altogether more acceptable home. Apart from the fact that it was without a garden, it was very suitable. This was certainly a miraculous provision from God and we were so grateful to the church for making it possible. We were all learning that God's ways are not our ways, and his plans, not our plans.

But the Kidderminster house remained unsold. What would happen when St. Andrew's needed their house back? Just when would the Kidderminster house sell? We parked these puzzles with God, and in the February of 1990 I departed on a two week trip to the USA and Canada, with my good friend Russ Parker.

It starts to dawn on us

While in the USA we visited the new base of Episcopal Renewal Ministries (the American equivalent of Anglican Renewal Ministries). The ERM team had decided to move away from their base on the East Coast to a new base in Denver, Colorado, so as to be more centrally placed in the country. They also had a suite of offices from which they worked with a staff of twenty. They were altogether more professional and efficient in their work than we. We were impressed by our meeting with Chuck Irish and Carl Buffington and others, and while I was there, God showed me a clearer vision of the work in England. I came back with two convictions in my mind. The first was that to become more effective, we would have to become more professional in the way we operated, without losing the personal and local touch that was so important in our work. To achieve this we would need to separate the work from the home and find larger offices. Secondly, we should consider moving to the geographical centre of the country, to signal that we and our services were available for churches in all parts of England, and to make travelling easier for me.

There was no sense in which I heard God clearly telling me to do this while I was in the USA, but it was more like a realisation of something obvious.

Julia, Bob, Sue, and the Trustees all felt that this would be a wise way to proceed. So now, we had to seek God for a new centre, a new office and of course we would now have to sell not only Bob and Sue's home, but also the house we lived in in Knaresborough. Around this time we also felt it right to pursue employing another member of staff to pioneer renewal amongst children. During this time Julia and I would meet regularly with Bob and Sue for prayer and waiting on God. These were very important times for us, and each time we met we found God speaking to us and encouraging us. More than once we found ourselves taken into places of repentance, not only for our own failings and lack of faith, but also for weaknesses in the wider church. At these times, God was giving us a growing sense of how he felt about the Church of England, and this gave us a deeper love and commitment to the church we had been called to serve.

By July we had not got very far on this, when I journeyed down to the John Wimber conference at

Holy Trinity Church, London which I mentioned in Chapter 6. We had now come to that point where we knew God was calling us to move, to expand the staff, but nothing was clear. However within the space of two days in London, God directed in two very clear ways.

Whilst at the Conference I bumped into Paul Corrie, Vicar of St. Alkmund's Church, Derby. I had not seen Paul since I was at St. John's College, Nottingham where we had both trained for the ordained ministry. In my prayers about a move of location, I had felt clearly God saying that we should first look for a church that would be a strong spiritual base for the Anglican Renewal Ministries team. I also felt him say that he had prepared this church, and we would recognise it by the enthusiastic reception they would give to the idea of our team joining the church.

I happened to mention to Paul that we were looking for a move. Without hesitation Paul said, 'You would be most welcome to come and join us in Derby.' At that stage Paul knew very little about Anglican Renewal Ministries and its work, and we really did not know each other very well. But there was a stirring of the Spirit within him, which was later shared by the PCC and leaders of the church, and to cut a long story short, it was not long before we were in no doubt that Derby was to be our new location.

The day after my meeting with Paul, I met with Alan Price in a café in central London and we shared our visions together. I was immensely excited by Alan's vision for children and suggested that he meet with the Anglican Renewal Ministries team and some of the Trustees. By mid-autumn the Trustees had appointed Alan to be a new full-time member of staff to work particularly with children.

All this was very exciting, but the mountains ahead of us now felt large and steep. Not least among our concerns was the state of our finances. In the autumn we launched an appeal to help cover the costs of the move to Derby, and to pay Alan's salary. But money was slow in coming in. Also Alan and his family had to find some money from somewhere to pay for a new home in Derby. On 23rd October, I wrote:

> As my anxiety levels have been growing lately, I have been given a word of encouragement from the Lord this morning through the lectionary reading, Luke 18:1–8. I must hold on to this, and to persevere in faith and loyalty. I feel almost haunted by Jesus' cry, 'When the Son of Man comes, will he find faith on the earth?' I have now got to walk by faith for the following:
> 1) The appeal – that God will provide for us financially.
> 2) The sale of the Knaresborough home.
> 3) The sale of Bob and Sue's house in Kidderminster.
> 4) To acquire a house for ourselves in Derby.
> 5) To acquire offices in Derby.
> 6) To find a house for Alan and Carol.

We then saw things starting to shift. The Trustees made the decision for Anglican Renewal Ministries to move to Derby in September. That very week a buyer became very interested in Bob and Sue's Kidderminster house and put in an offer. We hardly dared breathe! As the autumn progressed this became a firm offer and by the end of October, contracts had been signed and the house was released. As I wrote in my journal:

Praise the Lord! The sale of Bob and Sue's house has been a long trial indeed, but God has again proved himself utterly trustworthy, as the timing of this is marvellous. As I was thanking him, the text of Psalm 36:7 came to mind. I looked it up, and it reads, 'How priceless is your unfailing love!' Yes indeed, it is priceless.

The delay in the sale of Bob and Sue's house now made sense. God did not want them to buy a house in Knaresborough, only to sell it again a year later. He knew what he was doing.

Warfare and fasting

Although the Ashman's house had sold and we had seen houses in Derby for them and ourselves and the Prices and we had found suitable office accommodation, we could do absolutely nothing until the Anglican Renewal Ministries property that housed my family and the office had been sold. The signboard went up in September and the housing market was by now in deep recession. Added to this the appeal was still bringing in only a trickle.

A breakthrough came in November. I had asked Russ Parker to come and pray for us and listen with us. With his sharp gifts of discernment that I have learned to respect and trust, Russ detected that Anglican Renewal Ministries was in the grip of a considerable spiritual battle, and his perception was that the enemy had sent a particularly powerful and unpleasant demonic force to contest our right to exist. We discerned together that Satan's strategy for this was to cut off our supply lines of prayer and finance.

A few days after this we hosted a conference with

guest speakers Chris Woods and Bob Hopkins. One evening during this conference, they spoke on spiritual warfare, and they invited the conference to spend some time in warfare-prayer for us. I shall never forget that evening when one hundred and fifty people got to their feet, and all praying at once, did battle with the enemy, in prayer. I believe something broke in the heavenly places that night, for thereafter many were called to pray for us, and financial giving started to come in.

At this conference there was a Ugandan priest called John Magumba. He was in this country studying at Ridley Hall. We immediately warmed to this humble man of God, and giant of faith, and God used him to encourage me back into a discipline of fasting. So we returned from the conference considerably heartened and with a sense that we had heard God particularly about the need to fast and pray.

However, the see-saw of faith and fear continued. On 30th November I recorded;

Yesterday I was gripped by fear which almost overwhelmed me. Bob and I are very concerned about the state of our finances. Despite the appeal, we are very nearly broke and yet God keeps giving us these visions for expansion, extra staff etc. The fears flooded in and I am left wondering whether Anglican Renewal Ministries will really survive. But then last night's reading in Living Light took us back to Abraham: 'By faith Abraham, when God tested him, offered Isaac as a sacrifice. He who had received the promises was about to sacrifice his one and only son, even though God had said to him, "It is through Isaac that your offspring will be reckoned."' My 'Isaac' is Anglican Renewal

Ministries and I must be prepared to sacrifice it if God so wills, even if it apparently throws into jeopardy all the promises he has given us.

But, by the end of the year it was becoming clear that God did not want us to sacrifice our 'Isaac'. A very generous gift had come in which ensured our survival for a time at least.

In January, the sturdy Yorkshire house at 6 Scriven Road remained unsold despite prayers, fasting, and assurances by God. Our plan was to move at Easter (April) and time was getting short. I listened to God about this house. On January 4th, a day of prayer and fasting, I wrote:

> In a time of quiet, I felt God speak to me about 6 Scriven Road, and it is to do with spiritual warfare again. Satan's plan is to use this house to pin us down here and prevent us moving. As Jesus warned Peter ('Satan has tried to sift you like wheat'), so he warned me that Satan would try and destroy our faith through this. He would inflict despair, depression and anxiety. But we are to be warriors, not worriers and we are to mobilise the prayer troops into action about this. God wants us in Derby for April – that is his plan and we must go for that.

I spent time in prayer and fasting and releasing the house from any grip the enemy might have on it. The day after that, a couple came round and made an offer for the house. The offer was far too low but we managed to up it a little, still well below our asking price, but staff and Trustees felt that in the present climate it was right. On January 21st, I recorded my delight:

148

The house is now sold – PRAISE THE LORD! There is no doubt in my mind that this house has been sold as a direct result of prayer and fasting. We have also bought a house in Derby – Praise the Lord! Now we only have to get the office. God really is bringing all this together beautifully. In the autumn he spoke independently to both Julia and I, that we would move to Derby when the leaves returned to the trees. Our God is faithful.

During this time Bob and Sue had bought a new home, as did Alan and Carol. We also secured some office space reasonably priced and well-situated near the centre of Derby in a road called Friar Gate, which seemed suitably religious!

The end of one journey, and the start of another
Anyone who has been involved in house exchanges knows how precarious things feel until contracts have been exchanged. Despite so many assurances from God I had my nervous moments, and I felt it was right to continue with regular fasting and prayer to release the house. The day for exchanging contracts kept being delayed. However, the day came for the contracts to be signed and exchanged. My entry for 13th March:

Today we exchange contracts. The *Living Light* reading last night was predictably, 'Without faith it is impossible to please God'. My faith has been pitiful, but there is a mustard seed there, and God in his mercy has been able to respond even to this.

In the evening I wrote:

The contracts are signed and we are now free to move to Derby. Houses have been sold, and houses and offices found. God has been true to his promise, we shall move as the leaves return to the trees. Halleluia! Halleluia! Halleluia! The evening reading in Living Light: 'Be faithless no longer, believe!'

On Easter Sunday in 1991, the Mittons, the Ashmans and the Prices worshipped together at St. Alkmund's where they were welcomed by Paul Corrie and an enthusiastic church. I sang with a deeper conviction than normal, 'Jesus Christ is risen today, Halleluia'. So one journey had come to an end. It was for me, and for the Anglican Renewal Ministries team, one of ongoing lessons about hearing the sounds of God and trusting him with faith. A new journey began for us in Derby, and as I write this we have taken on another member of staff (administrative) and are increasing our office space. From time to time things feel fairly precarious financially, but we dare not forget all that we learned during that first journey of faith. As a team we continue to meet regularly and to listen to him and he keeps stirring us with new visions and challenges.

Notes

Chapter One

1 Michael Mitton, *The Wisdom to Listen*, Grove Pastoral Series 5, 1981.
2 I appreciate that there are church streams and spiritualities other than these three, but for the purposes of this book I have confined myself to these, not least because they are the ones that I am most familiar with.

Chapter Three

1 John Hadley, *Bread for the World* (DLT 1989) p.46.
2 op. cit. p.57.
3 I appreciate that some books are not quite in this category of reading. Commentaries, reports etc. will be necessary reading for different reasons.
4 David Runcorn, *Space for God* (Daybreak 1990) p.101.

Chapter Four

1 Gerard Manley Hopkins, *The Habit of Perfection* (Penguin 1953) p.5.
2 From R.S. Thomas', 'The Bright Field', in *Later Poems* (Papermac 1983) p.81.
3 Yevtushenko 'Autumn', in *Post-War Russian Poetry*, edited by Daniel Weissbort (Penguin 1974).
4 For futher reading see Brother Ramon's, *Deeper Into God*, and *Heaven on Earth*, both published by Marshall Pickering.
5 Christopher Bryant, *The River Within* (DLT 1978) p.73.
6 David Adam, *The Eye of the Eagle* (Triangle 1990) p.11.

7 Mark Stibbe, *Anglicans for Renewal*, Volume 49.
8 C.S. Lewis, *Letters to Malcolm*, ch.17 (quoted in above article).

Chapter Five
1 Russ Parker, *Healing Dreams* (SPCK 1988) p.7.
2 Herman Riffel, *Your Dreams, God's Neglected Gift* (Kingsway, 1984) p.22.
3 I include in this list that category of vision whereby we are enabled to see angels. Angels are all around us all the time, but we can only see and hear them when given the spiritual sight and hearing needed for supernatural things. Luke categorises Zechariah's meeting with an angel as a vision (Luke 1:22).

Mary (Luke 1:26–38): An angel comes to Mary to announce the news that she is to mother the Messiah.

Joseph (Matt. 1:20): An angel of the Lord appears to Joseph in a dream to announce Mary's pregnancy; Matt. 2:13: An angel of the Lord appears to him to tell him to flee with mother and child to Egypt.

Zechariah (Luke 1:11–22): An angel appears to him in the Temple to announce that he and Elizabeth are to have a child: John the Baptist.

Wise Men (Matt.2:12): they were warned in a dream not to go back to Herod.
4 A full account of this story can be found in *Anglicans for Renewal*, Summer 1992, p.10.
5 For those who wish to learn more about dreams, I would commend Russ Parker's book *Healing Dreams: Their Power and Purpose in Your Spiritual Life* (SPCK, London, 1989) and his cassette tape *Praying with Dreams, A Resource for Spiritual and Personal Growth* (Eagle, Guildford 1992). In

this cassette, Russ provides the listener with the background to start understanding dreams, to benefit from inner healing and use dreams in prayer. The double cassette includes seven sessions of 20–30 mins and includes one live counselling session in which a dream is used for inner healing and personal growth.

6 From David Adam's *The Edge of Glory* (Triangle 1985) part of the prayer *At Fire Lighting*, p.28.

7 Dietrich Bonhoeffer, *Letters and Papers from Prison* (SCM 1971) p.347.

8 George Herbert 'The Collar' included in *The English Poems of George Herbert*, selected by C A Patrides (J M Dent and Sons Ltd.1974).

9 Graham Kendrick, Make Way Music 1988. This hymn can be found in *Songs of Fellowship*, Kingsway Music, 1991, No. 604.

Chapter Six

1 For those not familiar with charismatic renewal, these are those gifts of the Spirit identified by St. Paul in 1 Cor. 12:10. Charismatics see these gifts as useful and readily available for the modern church.

2 1 Cor. 14:1 & 31.

3 In Marcel Driot's *Fathers of the Desert* (St. Paul Publications, UK 1992) p.25.

4 *The Age of Bede* (Penguin Classics 1988) pp. 43,44.

5 For this story see *The Age of Bede*, pp. 53,54.

6 James Ryle, *A Hippo in the Garden* (Highland 1992) pp.90, 91.

7 1 Cor. 14:29.

Chapter 7

1 David Adam, *Borderlands* (SPCK 1991) p.ix.

Exploring Prayer

*If you have found this book helpful, you may be
interested in other titles in this collection edited by
Joyce Huggett.*

Angela Ashwin
PATTERNS NOT PADDLOCKS

Prayer for parents and all busy people, suggesting
practical ideas and initiatives for prayer, building
on the chaotic, busy-ness of everyday life.

James Borst
COMING TO GOD

A stage by stage introduction to a variety of ways
of using times of stillness, quiet and contemplative
meditation.

Michael Mitton
THE SOUNDS OF GOD

Helpful hints on hearing the voice of God, drawn
from the contemplative, evangelical and
charismatic traditions.

Heather Ward
STREAMS IN DRY LAND

Praying when God is distant, when you feel bored
or frustrated with your prayer life – or even empty,
arid and deserted by God.

COMING IN SEPTEMBER 1993

Joyce Huggett
FINDING GOD IN THE FAST LANE

Gerald O'Mahony
FINDING THE STILL POINT